THE INFLUENCE OF A FATHER

THE INFLUENCE OF A FATHER

HOW YOU CAN BE THE
ROLE MODEL AND MENTOR
YOUR CHILDREN NEED

TOM LANE

Gateway Church
Southlake, Texas 76092

Gateway Church
500 S. Nolen, Suite 300
Southlake, Texas 76092
817-328-1000
influenceofafather@gatewaypeople.com

All examples involving ministry situations are real. However, the details and surrounding circumstances may have been altered or combined to preserve the privacy and confidentiality of the individuals involved.

For simplicity, the masculine pronoun is used when speaking in general terms; it is intended to be interchangeable with the feminine.

Cover design by Dean Wilder, Ellison Media Company, Phoenix, AZ.

All Scripture quotations are taken from the New King James Version (NKJV), copyright © 1979, 1980, 1982, Thomas Nelson, Inc., Publishers.

ISBN 0-9647435-4-X

10 9 8 7 6 5 4 3 2 1

Printed in the United States of America

This book is dedicated to my father, James Mitchell Lane; to my grandfathers, Harry Mitchell Lane and Newell A. Zuspan; and to my father-in-law, Dean Russell Frazier. The legacy of these fathers and their influence in my life continues on to bless future generations through my children, grandchildren and beyond them through all that are benefited by this book. The influence of a father cannot be overestimated!

Tom Lane

ACKNOWLEDGMENTS

This book would not have come about without the encouragement and support of my best friend, Jimmy Evans. Over the years, he has identified gifts in me and called them out, sometimes having to overcome my own resistance. I am forever blessed because of our friendship; it is a special gift from God that I do not take for granted. Thank you, Jimmy!

As I have written this book, my wife, and children have been constant sources of encouragement and support. I especially thank Jan for more than 32 years of love and commitment. She is my friend and partner, and without her there would be no stories to tell and no children to influence! Jan, you are the most wonderful gift God has given me!

I want to thank Todd, Lisa, Tyler, and Lindsay for allowing me to share our experiences. I am blessed by your love and I am overjoyed to see your response to God and His hand directing and blessing your lives. I have been overwhelmed with joy as I have watched you select your mate and begin your families. I am thankful for God's hand that is on your life and for the way you are raising your children. God's word is true! Jan and I now have the perspective of four generations of God's loving kindness to celebrate and reflect upon! Praise God!!!

There are many people who have contributed immeasurably to the completion of this project, its first printing and now this new reprint. Thanks to my secretary, Stephanie Evans, for all that she does in making me productive! Thank you to Kelly Hunt, who worked with me in the editing of this reprint. His insight and heart has helped me clarify my thoughts and added a deeper dimension to this reprint as it did in the first printing.

A special thanks to Kim LaNore and all my associates at Marriage Today for their hard work and commitment to the family. Finally, thanks to Ken Gire for his thoughtful consideration of my draft and his wise and experienced counsel on the original printing of this book.

I would be remise if I did not give thanks to the elders and congregation of Trinity Fellowship Church, who have loved me and have allowed the structure of ministry to accomplish great things for God including their extension of ministry through Gateway Church and my involvement there as God's plan continues to unfold. I appreciate the relationship that Trinity and Gateway hold in ministering together and I am thankful for the support of Gateway Elders and congregation as this effort to help men become the influence God has ordained for them continues to unfold.

TABLE OF CONTENTS

FOREWORD BY
JIMMY EVANS

I have known Tom Lane for over twenty years as my close personal friend and work associate. Without a doubt, he is the best father I know and has more authority to write a book on how to be a successful father than anyone I have ever known. His four children are living testimonies to his ability to use his influence as a father to raise terrific kids.

I have learned a great deal from Tom over the years in how to be a better parent. When I met him, I was in my mid-twenties and my children were very young. In watching Tom father his children, I was challenged and changed. My life and my children's lives have been deeply blessed by his example.

I encouraged Tom to write this book because of his obvious understanding on the subject and the great need that exists for men to learn to be good fathers. Many men in our society today have never had a father's influence in their life and therefore don't know what to do or how to do it in fathering their own children. For others, they have had a negative example from their own father and need to overcome it and learn positive parenting skills.

Whatever category you fall into, I highly recommend this book. In fact, I believe every mother would benefit from reading it also. Even though the subject is male oriented, these pages are filled with rich parenting skills that transcend gender.

Tom Lane is a great father. He has influenced my life in a profound way. I am grateful to God for putting him in my path as my dear friend. I am also thankful that he has written this book to touch all of us with his rich insights on how to be successful fathers.

Jimmy Evans

INTRODUCTION

The Heritage of a Father:
The Gift That Keeps on Giving

*Accomplishments and material
things are temporary at best; measure
your success in life by the legacy you
leave through your children.*

"I never knew the extent of God's love for me until I was 44 years old," one man told me recently. He did not understand God's love because it had not been properly represented in his home or reflected in his relationship with his father. He is fortunate to have overcome this deficit so that a new cycle of blessing could be established in his family as he reveals God's love to his children.

As a pastor I have discovered that most people are not aware of how much of an influence their fathers' presence or absence has had on them, whether negative or positive. To be a successful father, one must have a pattern to follow—a model to copy. In order to be a successful father himself, a man must have been fathered successfully or must have another source from which to be trained. Sadly, our society offers very little solid resource in this area.

For those seeking answers, there is an ominous "black hole" when it comes to instruction about fatherhood. The bookstores are packed with alternative methods seeking to fill the void of instruction; unfortunately, many espouse various lifestyles that do not consider God. But God's method is time-tested and proven to produce results that bring blessing to families and change the course of nations.

There are others more academically qualified to speak on the issues of child development. As I pen these words, it is my purpose in this book to share my childhood experiences and how they have shaped my life. It is out of my childhood and family experiences that I have come to know God and through knowledge of Him I have formed my parenting philosophies. I am a father of four children, all of them now adults. My family was an intact family. My parents were married over 40 years. My dad was a great dad and he imparted to me fathering skills that I have applied to the parenting of my children. My parenting story is not a story of "my kids went to Hell and this is how I got them back." Mine is a story of faithfulness—God's faithfulness to me and my faithfulness to Him.

I have sought to love God and serve him with my whole heart and to influence my children to do the same. My purpose in this book is to tell how my father, grandfathers, and father-in-law have influenced my life, and how I took their influence and coupled it with my love for God to train and prepare my children for life.

In the pages ahead, I attempt to provide practical information and instruction for men who want to assume their role as an influential father to their children. If you don't know how to assume that role in your children's lives because you have not had that influence in your own life, this book is for you!

My prayer is that, through sharing my experiences and the principles I have learned, families will be strengthened and fathers will become effective in their God-ordained call to lead and influence their children.

A boy needs a father to train him in godly character and responsibilities. He needs a role model to prepare him for his role as a father. Likewise, a young girl needs guidance to know what to expect from her husband in his role as husband and father of her family. She needs to see the model first in her father.

God's plan calls for children to be trained in the home and to pass their knowledge from generation to generation. In fact, over the last 6,000 years, God's plan has been available through His prophets and teachers, and His plan is still available to mankind as recorded in the Bible.

The social ills we are experiencing have their roots in our failure as fathers. It is clear to me that a father's influence cannot be overestimated as it relates to forming character, transferring values, and leading his children into a dynamic personal relationship with God.

My life is a testimony of the power of positive influence from a father. I am fortunate to have fond memories of my childhood. Simply stated, my dad was a great father. His presence was an influential factor in my development as a man. From his father, he learned and incorporated for himself the direction, discipline, and affirming attention necessary to provide the foundation for a stable home. Like his father had done with him, he demonstrated his love to me with hugs, consistent positive behavior, and words of affirmation. He knew that little eyes were watching.

I am his product; and I have incorporated his model into my parenting philosophy, a philosophy that is anchored in the belief that children are a gift from God (Psalm 127:3). What we model and transfer to our children through our behavior must be a reflection of God and His plans for our life and theirs. As such, we must approach fatherhood with the same diligence as the builders of the Empire State building. We must lay a solid foundation. We

> *What you model and transfer to your children through your behavior must be a reflection of God and His plans for your life and theirs.*

must add bricks of truth and character consistently with utmost care and integrity. Most importantly, we must build as God, the master architect, intended.

The cornerstone of my parenting philosophy is the principle of transference. Using this principle, I have set out to lead and influence my children—Todd, Lisa, Tyler, and Lindsay. Because of this principle I have the full expectation that they will pass on to their children the values I have modeled and molded into them. This system of influence is the method God intended parents to use as they build and prepare the next generation. It is a system based on the principle of transference. The important truth represented in the principle of transference forms the hub that all other issues of parenting influence revolve around.

The principle of transference is the idea that we will transfer to our children the values and character demonstrated from our life. In other words our values must be modeled by our own behavior if we want them to transfer to our children. When we understand this principle we realize that our actions are a much more influential tutor than the instruction of our words or the concepts we believe but do not practice.

Through 23 years of pastoral counseling experience, I have come to understand that not everyone has as fond memories of childhood as I do. Many suffer, even as adults, from a childhood filled with abandonment, violence, and abuse. Others suffer from neglect and hurt, the result of fathers who were distracted or disinterested. Many simply suffer from a lack of Biblical training in the household. Tragically, this flow of hurt and dysfunction continues and multiplies from one generation to the next.

Whatever your background, I want you to know that it is never too late to start. Perhaps you are overwhelmed at the responsibility of being a father. Or, perhaps you are paralyzed by fear because you have little or no training for fatherhood. That is quite common. Fortunately, God specializes in rewarding latecomers. *"I wish to give to this last man the same as to you,"* was the statement by the owner of the vineyard to the workers. This statement was made in a parable that Jesus told (Matthew 20:14) referring to God's system of reward for those who come to him. The vineyard owner enlisted workers to work later in the day and paid them the same as those who worked all day—even though they had not worked as long or as hard as the others.

No doubt it is best to understand your role as father before you have children. However, even if it is late in your parenting day, meaning your children are grown or almost grown, the good news is that you can still implement God's principles, and as you implement them you make Him a partner in your effort.

Even if your parenting story is not like mine and you are looking for a way to call your children back from potentially tragic situations, the principles we discuss in this book will give you tools that will help. Regardless of your current situation your efforts to learn and apply God's principles will produce good fruit and blessing for your children.

God has given men the high calling of *fatherhood.*

Greater than any business or ministry accomplishment, with the power to accomplish more than Bill Gates' fortune, is the potential influence a father has to a thousand generations (Exodus 20:6).

Join me in the coming pages for a practical discussion related to your influence as a father. God's promises are real. His blessings are eternal. It is worth the effort to learn and apply God's principles to our own lives, so that through the principle of transference we can become influential fathers to our children and to our children's children. In doing so, you can experience God's blessing in your family through multiple generations. Scripture is true when it states, "His loving kindness is better than life!!!" I hope you will find much of value in the chapters ahead and be able to apply what you read to your life for the benefit of your family and your influence as a father.

CHAPTER 1

Taking a Personal Inventory

*Your goal must be to transfer to your children
a dynamic relationship with a living God,
Who created you and loves you.*

After teaching a course about God, a university professor made a startling discovery.

On the first day of class, the professor had asked his students to answer questions—in writing—about their relationship with their fathers. *How does your father exact discipline? How does your father express his love to you? What actions on your part make your father proud? What actions disappoint your father?*

At semester's end, after months of Biblical teaching about God's attributes and His unfailing love for mankind, the professor again asked his students to answer questions…similar to the first, but with a twist. This time, the subject was God. *How do you believe that God exacts discipline? How does God express His love to you? What actions on your part make God proud? What actions disappoint God?*

Upon comparison, the professor discovered that his students' perception of God was *a direct reflection* of their relationship with their fathers! The moral: *A father's influence determines a child's view of God more than a whole semester of in-depth study, full of Bible truths!*

Although unscientific, I submit that the results of this informal poll ring true. To be successful fathers, we must demonstrate God's nature to our children. We cannot simply shift the responsibility to our spouses, their Sunday school teachers, or other people of influence in their life. We must have a "Day of Reckoning" to accept for ourselves the fact that as fathers, we have a profound influence on the outcome of future generations.

A father's influence has a "ripple effect." As a stone thrown into a pond, our influence produces ripples, which impact our sons and daughters, washing over them, circling ever larger across future generations. These ripples will affect every area of our children's lives including the persons they choose to marry, their education, their personal and professional accomplishments, how they handle finances, their ability to make quality friends, and eventually where they will spend eternity.

As such, our goal should not be merely to raise "politically correct" children to become religious adults who will fit well into society. Rather, our goal should be to rear children of purpose, who understand that they are uniquely important in the eternal scheme of things, children who comprehend that true satisfaction in life is only found in the recognition of God's deliberate work and purpose.

Accomplishing this is not a shallow religious act, nor is it a duty of good citizenship, as if the transferring of knowledge forms the

> *Your goal should be to rear children of purpose who understand that they are uniquely important in the eternal scheme of things.*

basis for fulfillment and purpose. It must be our goal to transfer to our children a dynamic relationship with a living God, Who created us and loves us. The transfer of this relationship happens through personal involvement of the heart and soul, and is reflected in a total commitment of our person.

To lay the foundation for a relationship with God in our children, we must first understand two foundational truths:

1. God is the creator and owner of all things.
2. Man's purpose and destiny is only fully found in service and surrender to Him.

Only with a complete understanding of these truths can we effectively represent God's nature to our children.

Truth #1: God is the Creator and Owner of All Things

On January 22, 1973, the United States Supreme Court made a fundamentally flawed decision that unleashed gigantic and tragic waves of immorality across our country. The case was Roe vs. Wade, in which the high court legalized abortion on demand. The outcome of this decision has eliminated greater numbers of people than the 6 million Jews systematically murdered during the holocaust of World War II[1]. Since 1973, approximately 38 million abortions have been performed in the United States, a number more than double the 1990 population of the five largest cities in America.[2]

The court's premise for the decision was that human sexual activity, in itself, produces a pregnancy. It further concluded that sexuality is under the sole control of the individuals participating in the sexual act. On this logic, the court ruled that it is a woman's right to decide the outcome of her pregnancy.

The Bible exposes the flaw of this reasoning in its clear portrayal of God as Creator, at work in the womb to form us. Based on the Bible's revelation, it is clear that birth is not an accident. His hand guides the biological process of conception so that each person is the product of God's will and work. Life is God's determination, not man's choice. Even to the nonbeliever, this is evident in the fact that all over the earth, even with a world population approaching 7 billion, each person's fingerprints are different—*on each finger!*—completely formed in the womb in the sixth month. Each one of us is unique, a product of God's design.

Psalm 139:13-16 says:
> *"For You formed my inward parts;*
> *You covered me in my mother's womb…*
> *My frame (or bones) was not hidden from You,*
> *When I was made in secret,*
> *And skillfully wrought in the lowest parts of the earth.*
> *Your eyes saw my substance, being yet unformed.[3]*
> *And in Your book they all were written,*
> *The days fashioned for me,*
> *When as yet there were none of them."*

And Job 10:8 says:
> *"Your hands have made me and fashioned me,*
> *An intricate unity…"*

And God told Jeremiah in Jeremiah 1:5:
> *"Before I formed you in the womb I knew you;*
> *Before you were born I sanctified you;*
> *And I ordained you a prophet to the nations."*

God knows every person's weaknesses, and He factors even our weakness into His divine plans. When God called Moses to lead the children of Israel out of Egypt, Moses objected, citing slow speech as his reason, God answered:

> *"Who has made man's mouth? Or who makes the mute, the deaf, the seeing, or the blind? Have not I, the LORD?"* (Exodus 4:11)

God is the creator of all things and the Bible tells us that all things were created by Him to fulfill His purposes, Colossians 1:16 says:

> *"For by Him all things were created that are in heaven and that are on the earth, visible and invisible, whether thrones or dominions or principalities or powers. All things were created through Him and for Him."*

In treating birth as a right of human choice, the Supreme Court erred. The court failed to acknowledge two vital truths: first—God is Creator of everything, second—as His creation, mankind is ultimately accountable to Him. In short, the Supreme Court is not supreme; God created all things, animate and inanimate. Therefore, He is the rightful owner of all creation, and we are responsible to Him for our actions.

Understanding these two foundational truths: that God is the creator and owner of all things, and that we are responsible to him for our actions should radically sharpen a father's view of his parenting role. Suddenly, he realizes that procreation is God-centered, not human-centered. Life is a gift. God has divinely initiated this birth, guided development in the womb, and entrusted the gift to me!

The second truth builds on the first and calls for a personal response of commitment.

Truth #2: *Man's Purpose and Destiny is Only Found in Service and Surrender to God*

An awareness of God has always been a part of my life. He was discussed at our dinner table. He was honored on Sunday. And although I could not see Him, my parents and grandparents demonstrated through their actions that He was a real Person, very much alive and a central part of our home life.

My family attended church out of gratitude toward God not out of fear that failure to acknowledge Him might evoke His wrath. We regarded the Bible as worthy of lifelong study, considering it a privilege to gain a greater knowledge of God and His ways. We prayed regularly, humbling ourselves in service to Him. We freely gave time and money to the church, helping others with no expectation of acknowledgement or reward. God was the issue—not benevolence, not humanitarian service, not social etiquette.

As a result, my parents set forth an example of a living, breathing relationship with a Supreme Being. Naturally, almost effortlessly, they transferred this concept to me—not only in words, but also by consistent actions. Based on the important principle of transference, what my parents had in their own life and lived consistently they were able to transfer to me.

Their example served as the foundation for a very important decision I made at age 16. At that point in my life, God became more than a religious concept to me. He used circumstances to break through my insensitivity and suddenly, I was aware of Him; I knew He was there and it was more than an awareness of religious knowledge or tradition as I'd had before. I understood that He was offering me a one-on-one relationship with Him. Fortunately, my father, (future) father-in-law, and my grandfathers had shown me the way. They did not see the pursuit of God as something for preachers, women, children, and elderly men. They led the way and their leadership made it easy for me at age 16 to surrender my life to Jesus Christ. Through my personal act of surrender, God became alive and real to me. More than a concept, He became my friend, savior, and Lord.

Without my father's influence I might live as many men today, viewing God only in religious terms or not viewing Him at all, holding to the opinion that religion is for preachers, the elderly, women, and children. *Real men do not need God*, goes the mindset.

From this perspective, many men of today see God as a weakness and a crutch rather than the Supreme Creator, who is the source of true power and success. And yet, a father will not be fully effective as a leader and teacher to his children without acknowledging God in the entire process of life. Proper values and character in their truest and purest form are only found in God. Apart from Him, the values and principles of character we try to transfer either become diluted, or they simply do not transfer at all. The teaching and training we give to our children will never measure up if we simply say to our children, "Follow me, I know the way, I alone am the model." If we remove God from our parenting, we will miss the mark in developing our children to their fullest potential.

Many fathers today already understand that their model is not a good one, but they mistakenly believe they have nothing else to offer. And yet, no father wants to tell his son: "Do not live like me. Be like your friend's father." I believe that every father desires in his heart to leave an enduring legacy, one in which his children will experience an overflowing measure of fulfillment, purpose, and destiny.

You must have a personal relationship with God to be able to transfer it to your children!

So, we must first take inventory of our lives. The principle of transference reminds us that we cannot transfer to our children what we do not have. It only makes sense to begin with our own relationship with God as we consider how to raise our children.

A Concluding Thought

Based on the discussion in this chapter, I hope you agree and recognize with me that God created our children with unique gifts to fulfill God's plan. He created them; they belong to Him and they have been entrusted to us to be developed to their full potential and purpose through our influence. We cannot introduce our children to God and help them discover His plan and purpose for their life without knowing Him ourselves. *We must have a personal relationship with God to be able to transfer it to our children!*

Where are you today? Is God a religious concept? Or is He an important part of your life, as demonstrated daily through a living relationship?

Hebrews 11:6 tells us:

> *"...for he who comes to God must believe that He is, and that He is a rewarder of those who diligently seek Him."*

In other words, a person must first believe that God exists; and secondly, that God promises to reward those who make a steady, earnest effort to find Him.

And what is the reward? Romans 6:23 says:

> *"For the wages of sin is death, but the gift of God is eternal life in Christ Jesus our Lord."*

The reward of diligently seeking God is finding abundant life— in this world as well as in all eternity. That life is found only through God's Son, Jesus Christ, who said:

> *"I am the way, the truth, and the life. No one comes to the Father except through Me."* (John 14:6)

We cannot work our way to God with charitable deeds (Romans 3:23). We cannot serve our way to Him through religious dedication (Titus 3:5). We can only come to Him through an acknowledgement that our best efforts to be good and please Him have failed. By doing so, we agree with Him, opening the door to accept His offer of forgiveness.

In a nutshell, that is the Gospel. Jesus Christ died for us so that we might have restoration, forgiveness, abundant spiritual life, and intimacy with God. When we accept this truth, God becomes more than a concept. He becomes real and walks with us each day. As a result, He enables us to live as a positive role model to our children, leading them in the footsteps of Christ.

Every person will make one of two decisions in their life; one is to accept Jesus Christ as personal Savior and Lord and receive the benefits of a relationship with Him. The other is to reject His offer of relationship and choose to live life by self-fashioned rules. Rejection of Him brings its own penalty and sabotages the influence God intended for fathers to have on their children. I encourage you to be bold and accept Christ today.

He is the source of power and success. The response you make is the single most important decision and action you will take in your life. The influence of a father begins with the decision to be influenced by truth and the claim of God in a personal way. Do not wait; act now.

Romans, Chapter 10 tells us that we believe with our heart, but with the mouth confession is made unto salvation. Pray this life-changing prayer out loud:

> *"Jesus, I confess that I am a sinner. All my efforts to be good and please You have failed. I thank You that You paid the price for my sins. I ask you to forgive me, come into my life, and make me new inside. With your daily help, I will follow you for the rest of my life. Amen"*

In your heart, you surrendered your life to Christ and as you spoke aloud the prayer above and you made confession to your own salvation.

The step you have taken will allow God to change you and develop His character and values in your life. He will empower you to live your life for Him and enable you to transfer His work in your life to your children, becoming the father of influence that He intends for you to be.

CHAPTER 2

Understanding the Nature of Your Child

As precious and unique as each child is, we must not forget that there is Foolishness bound up in his or her little heart.

"Foolishness is bound up in the heart of a child..."

Proverbs 22:15

Foolish acts make no sense to the logical mind. They lack forethought, wisdom, and the appropriate measure of caution. Every person I see in counseling wants their actions to be evaluated based on what was intended by the action, rather than the result. Rarely do they extend the same grace when evaluating others actions. Adults relate this way in their relationships, and when they become parents, they relate this way to their children. Even though we'd like to be judged by our intentions, we often become frustrated and impatient when we catch our children in some act of foolishness. We ignore their intent and focus on their behavior.

Wise fathers understand that their children will do things that make no sense, lack forethought, and have no measure of wisdom or caution associated with them. The foolish behavior of our children is an opportunity to discover their intent and teach our values because by our reactions, we can show them how to use forethought and draw on their own experience or the wisdom of others before acting.

The Bible is very clear about this matter related to children. It tells us to expect children to act foolishly—to not be surprised by their foolish behavior. When faced with our children's foolishness it encourages us to diligently train them and lovingly correct their foolish actions.

Every one of us could tell stories of the childish, foolish, even stupid things we have done. Foolishness is not a respecter of personality, social class, ethnicity, or religious belief…nor is it a respecter of authors who write books on fatherhood.

Summertime, 1960: It was the middle of a long, hot day in Omaha, Nebraska, and I was bored. Homework and the rigid schedule of third grade were long forgotten. I needed excitement—something different to break the monotony.

Then it hit me: I would build something.

In the garage, I searched the scrap pile for wood and my dad's workbench for tools. I couldn't find his regular claw hammer so I grabbed the next best thing, his ball peen hammer, a funny-looking hammer with a fat, rounded end, designed for shaping metal or for pounding-out dents.

I set up shop on the front porch, a four-foot square slab of concrete just the right size for this 8-year-old to hammer and saw and nail. I don't remember what I set out to build; I just remember that I was excited to have everything that I needed.

Eagerly, I cut several boards and started nailing them together with the ball peen hammer. I had hammered several nails into the boards when one of the swings went awry, missed the nail, and ricocheted off the board. With cat-like reflexes, my foot jerked out of the way of the uncontrolled hammer as it knocked a circular concrete chunk from the porch's front edge. Suddenly, all interest in the construction project left me; I was mesmerized by the hammer's work on the edge of the concrete porch.

For the next half-hour, I centered my attention on the porch, knocking out concrete chunks to create a jagged edge, and then tapping each to make it uniform. The creative genius of my work was intoxicating.

Down the street, one of my friends saw me hammering away and walked over for a look. He examined the litter of broken concrete, the jagged porch and asked me, "What are you *doing*?!"

I was brought to a full awareness of my foolishness as I explained how I got started knocking chunks off the edge of the porch.

I went flush when he exclaimed, "When your dad gets home, he is gonna *kill* you!"

First reality set in; then panic. There I stood a mixture of awe and terror, struggling to find a way to undo my destructive work.

To my surprise, when my dad came home, he did not ground me for life, nor give me something more physically impressionable to underscore his displeasure. To be sure, he was disappointed and frustrated. He asked for an explanation: "What were you thinking?"

"I don't know-w-w!" My voice had turned into the whine of a child caught in a foolish act.

Nevertheless, my dad, who was well aware of the cost to fix a broken porch, did not focus on the cost of my action. It would have been easy for my dad to lecture me on the stupidity of my behavior. I'm sure it must have been tempting to rub my nose in the fact that my actions had absolutely no forethought. And due to my lack of caution, I failed to consider the consequences of my action. He would have felt justified to administer painful punishment to teach me the lesson of my life—one that I would never forget.

To my amazement, even to this day, my dad did not raise his voice as he talked to me about my stunt. He did not have to convince me of the foolishness of my action. Instead, he made me walk with him through the steps of repairing the porch. As I became aware of all that was involved in fixing the damage done by my foolishness, I came face to face with the consequences of my actions. Although the cost of the repair was well beyond my ability to pay, my dad saw to it that I made some level of restitution by sacrificing my allowance and some of my savings. He fit the punishment to my maturity level and my level of sacrifice to my age and ability.

Even as adults, there are times when despite our best effort to avoid foolishness, it finds us. For instance, we are confronted with this reality when an officer approaches our car window and declares his radar has clocked us exceeding the speed limit, and asks, "Is there an emergency?" We can hear ourselves ramble some inane excuse, and suddenly what made perfect sense just a few minutes earlier makes no logical sense when presented to the officer. Even when we

A successful father is one who is able to correct the foolish behavior without inflicting emotional hurt.

chide ourselves with personal rebukes like, "*You should know better,*" it does not solve the dilemma created by our foolishness as adults, nor will it properly train or correct our children's foolish behavior.

Our children's potential is in our hands as it relates to taming the negative instincts and cultivating the positive virtues within them. This is the reality of responsible parenting, and no father can succeed without understanding the capacity for foolishness common to all men. A successful father is one who is able to correct the foolish behavior without inflicting emotional hurt. Accomplishing this is like mastering any other skill. *It is not difficult to do, once you know how.*

Corrective discipline is the means to address the foolish nature in our children. The purpose of discipline is always redemptive. God does not intend for it to be abusive, destructive, or harsh. Loving concern for the development of the child should motivate all discipline.

A father's proactive and positive response to the foolish behavior of his children will determine whether the correction will produce the desired result. If the response is uncaring, negative, or rejecting toward the children, their foolish nature goes uncorrected, leading to a life of behavioral dysfunction that imbeds into their thinking and responses. The dysfunction remains with them, producing unhealthy fruit even as adults.

In Chapter Seven, I will discuss in detail the proper methods for discipline. For now, let me say that for these methods to be effective, we must avoid three common tendencies.

Tendency # 1: *To Reject the Child Along with His Behavior*

Men often respond to foolishness with verbal and physical abuse—doing and saying things that scar children for life, such as labeling them as *stupid* or *failures.* A father lashing out to instill fear in his children does not "scare away" the foolishness. In fact, quite the opposite happens. The foolish nature imbeds even deeper, leaving the child with scars of rejection. Confused and rejected, the child must now sort out life without the guidance of corrective discipline.

When a child's foolish nature appears in some action or behavior, a father should never express dissatisfaction through rejection. Neither should we expect their foolish nature to evaporate without the diligent care of corrective discipline. The successful father gives loving acceptance to his children while correcting the foolishness of their behavior.

Every father must realize that God gives him a naturally foolish child at birth. The Bible is clear about this. Proverbs 22:15 tells us:

"Foolishness is bound up in the heart of a child..."

Even though this statement is true, children also have tremendous, God-given potential, unique to them. Sometimes, a child's silliness is so cute, we can't help but laugh; sometimes, it is expensive (as in the cost of repairing a jagged concrete porch); often,

> ## *The successful father gives loving acceptance to his children while correcting the foolishness of their behavior.*

it is extremely frustrating. Whether cute, expensive, or frustrating—we must realize that our attitude and the discipline we administer will determine whether a child overcomes his or her natural foolishness.

Foolishness is not about knowledge, I.Q., or genetics. It is about the sin nature common to man. Regardless of intellect, abilities, or personalities, we are all infected with the curse of a naturally rebellious and foolish nature, which began with Adam and Eve's fall (Genesis 3). This nature struggles with the wonderful virtues of God, imparted to us through the instruction of our parents. It is critical that, as parents, we correct the foolishness that is the seedbed for sin and cultivate the character of God and His virtues in our children so that His nature prevails in their natural attitudes and their foolish actions.

As an answer to the foolishness, the reminder of Proverbs 22:15 says:

"...The rod of correction will drive it far from him."

The wisdom expressed by Solomon in this quote brings

understanding to our children's negative behavior so that we can deal with it in a positive manner. God's solution for subduing sin and promoting righteousness is wise, caring parents, who understand the true nature of their children and who respond with loving discipline. Foolishness should not be the cause for rejection or for expecting the silly nature to somehow evaporate without diligent care.

I look back with great admiration upon my father and his handling of the broken porch incident. At this foolishness, many fathers might have reacted improperly, perhaps responding with abusive words, harsh punishment, or rejection. My father corrected me for my foolishness, but was aware that foolish actions are part of the training process between a father and his children. To this day, I bear the lasting fruit of my father's loving influence and his response of correction to my many acts of childhood foolishness. His response was always loving and proper.

Tendency #2: *To Delegate the Discipline*

Men often delegate discipline to the wife or someone else. As a counselor, I frequently hear this excuse: "I am gone all day at work. I don't want to be the heavy when I get home."

When a man sees the role of disciplinarian as "the heavy," it is usually because that is the way his dad administered discipline in his life. He recoils as a result of his own experience with discipline and removes himself from discipline situations with his children. This response opens the door for fear to take root, the paralyzing fear of becoming verbally or physically abusive. Because of the power of their personality or physical strength, men often convince themselves that someone gentler and less physical should administer correction.

In reality, nothing could be further from the truth. God has established the father as the doorkeeper of the home. Whatever the father tolerates will be tolerated; whatever he resists will be systematically rooted out. Notice that Ephesians 6:4 specifically addresses fathers:

"And you, fathers, do not provoke your children to wrath, but bring them up in the training and admonition of the Lord."

Men are to be the initiators of discipline and teaching in the home. This isn't to say that women aren't equal to men or that they are less important in the development of the children. It is to say that the Bible commands the father to lead. A father must support and reinforce the discipline administered by the mother. Unity between husband and wife is an important factor necessary for the correction to be fully effective.

When a father delegates the responsibility for discipline to his wife and she is passive or refuses to administer discipline, the negative effect is compounded in the children. In this case, the foolish behavior is never addressed, leaving the child to self-develop. The results are dysfunctional behavior patterns, which affect every area of life—all because the father won't apply the Biblical mandate and bring correction to the foolish nature of his child.

I watched a young man in our church self-develop like this. His dad is a hard-working man whose job takes him away from home many weeks. However, he always attempts to be home on the weekends. In his early teens the young boy was taller and stronger than his mother, and although she tried to correct him when he got out of line, she had no means of enforcement. When her husband was in town on the weekends, he did not want to strain his relationship with his kids by enforcing correction, so he did not discipline his son, and his wife could not administer the discipline she knew was necessary because her son was too big.

This young man struggled with authority at school and could not keep a job. The wrong crowd of friends influenced his behavior and it grieved his mom and dad. Although they did not agree with what he was doing, they failed to correct his behavior with discipline and he was left to self-develop. As a young adult he lacks purpose and direction, and he continues to lead a life dominated by foolish behavior.

Every woman that I know loves for her husband to be proactive in the children's lives. When women are released from the unfair burden of "doing the dirty work," as discipline is sometimes thought, a beautiful thing happens: security and freedom emerge in the marriage, love is in the air, and children become the *"peaceable fruits of righteousness,"* as stated in Hebrews 12:11:

> *"Now no chastening (or discipline) seems to be joyful for the present, but painful; nevertheless, afterward it yields the peaceable fruit of righteousness to those who have been trained by it."*

Tendency #3: *To Project Unrealistic Expectations*

Men learn through experience that to succeed, you must produce results. This pressure to produce often leads to self-imposed standards of performance and unrealistic expectations in their lives. It also can be the catalyst for unrealistic expectations of perfection to be placed upon their children. When this happens the result is long-term emotional damage.

As adults, we do not hold up under the pressure of these expectations, and neither do our children. Correcting foolishness is a process. No potter expects instant results from his lump of clay; he establishes in his mind's eye the end result he desires, and skillfully crafts his piece of clay into the work he envisions. Likewise, a father must establish the vision and values that will govern the activities of his home. Through patient, skillful work he carefully molds his vision and values into the lives of his children, producing a treasure for God.

My friend, Jimmy Evans, tells a story of a man he counseled who lacked confidence in any new situation and was paralyzed with a fear of failure. As they worked to discover the source of this man's fear, the man very reluctantly revealed a situation of hurt from his childhood. When this grown man was 8 years old he went to the garage to be with his dad who was doing repair work on the family car. He was standing beside the car listening and watching his dad while he worked underneath the car. His dad called out to him to get him the crescent wrench off his workbench, but the young boy did not know what a crescent wrench was so he took a guess and grabbed a random tool. When he handed it to his dad, his dad threw it across the garage and yelled at him, calling him stupid and cursing him for not getting the right tool. He finally ended his verbal tirade with the phrase, "if you don't know any more than this, get out of my garage, and go help your mother in the house where you belong." The man was devastated by his father's words and his own inability to live up to his father's expectations. The scar of this event stuck with him through his growing up years and as an adult was replayed in his mind as he encountered new situations. His insecurity and fear was linked to this experience. He never again

A father must have compassion, vision, patience, and a steadfast commitment to the process of preparing and molding his child's life with positive and corrective reinforcement.

wanted to experience the rejection he had experienced from his father when he failed to meet his expectations. So he was trapped in fear and insecurity unable to approach new situations with confidence.

How else is a boy to be taught, if not by involvement with a father who has realistic expectations for his student? A father's role is not that of resident potentate to be served by a crew of servant children. Instead, a father must be a trainer, equipper, motivator, mentor, and coach. A father must have compassion, vision, patience, and a steadfast commitment to the process of preparing and molding his child's life with positive and corrective reinforcement.

As trainer, he imparts to his children the fundamentals for behavior. As equipper, he prepares his children for service by providing the necessary resources for the work. As motivator, he inspires and challenges his children to achieve what is thought of as impossible. As mentor, he shows his children the way by highlighting the principles that apply to each situation, having himself walked the path of preparation. As coach, he evaluates the progress, correcting his children through positive interaction when they miss the mark.

There is no higher purpose for a father than to develop the full potential of his children so that their lives are consumed with love and service to God.

In Chapter Seven, I will offer specific steps to help you accomplish the positive work of discipline in your children. However, in the chapters between now and then, I want to present the big picture, the bird's eye view of fatherhood, so that when you arrive at the chapters on discipline, you will understand the true purpose for discipline, and the treasure it produces in the lives of your children. With this perspective you will be able to successfully shape the character of your children and avoid the mistakes that will prevent you from influencing your children as God designed.

A Concluding Thought

As we have talked through the pages of this chapter, I believe God has been with you as you've been reading. Through the gentle work of His presence, I believe He has been making specific application to you of the material presented, personalizing it through situations from your own family.

Are you frustrated by your children's imperfections? Have you shifted the burden of correction to your wife, or to someone else? Do you resent your children's foolish behavior, or perhaps harbor unrealistic expectations about their development apart from your careful and patient input? Are you recognizing in a new way that parenting is a process?

These are tough questions to ask and even tougher ones to face.

The Bible tells us that imperfection is woven into the human fabric, to be removed only through proper correction over a period of time. The remedy begins with an understanding of the nature of children, and continues with a commitment to the corrective process. Removing unrealistic expectations and accepting your responsibility to provide vision, values, and discipline for your children empowers them to step into God's perfect plan for their lives. This is the guarantee for God's blessing now and into the future.

Why not be honest with God today, and acknowledge your need for His help? James 1:5 says:

> "If any of you lacks wisdom, let him ask of God, who gives to all liberally and without reproach, and it will be given to him."

The phrase "without reproach" in this verse means "without mocking, ridiculing, or using angry or sarcastic words." God is merciful and gives wisdom without reminding us of our unworthiness.

Why not acknowledge any areas of shortcoming and initiate a discussion with your wife regarding the changes necessary in you and with your family? When two are in agreement, God is released to do His most miraculous work.

Although foolishness is a part of a child's nature, correction will drive that foolishness far away and in the process produce a beautiful treasure for God! It takes a diligent, faith-filled father to lead the effort, partnering with his wife, to produce the result we are describing. The partnership will produce the fullest result in your children. Why not work with your spouse to apply the principles we have discussed in this chapter. The results will not come quickly, but they will be awesome!

CHAPTER 3

Influencing Your Children
Toward Godliness

*In our home, we successfully imparted
our values to our children
in a positive atmosphere of
fun and celebration.*

Author Thomas Carruthers once said, "A teacher is one who makes himself progressively unnecessary." So it is with successful parents: their daily guidance and oversight become unnecessary as they skillfully transfer their values and beliefs to their children.

In this chapter, I offer some practical insight, along with tools to make the transfer of godliness and moral character to your children a natural part of your family life. By presenting my solutions to some commonly shared parenting struggles, my experience can work to your advantage by allowing you to learn from my experiences. As Thomas Edison said, "I have not failed; I've just found 10,000 ways that won't work." He made that statement on his way to inventing one of the greatest innovations ever to benefit man, the light bulb.

Before we talk about methods, we must first ask ourselves, "What am I trying to transfer?" We can only transfer those things that we possess, whether physical or spiritual. Our children will only accept from us what we are actively experiencing in our lives and therefore are modeling for them. So let's take an honest look at ourselves, and ask some pointed questions. First, define your relationship with God, is it personal and intimate? Or is it religious and impersonal, formal and works-oriented, or legalistic and rules-centered. An impersonal relationship with God produces a life that is void of spiritual vibrancy. God's values are time honored and unchanging. They are not based on what seems right in given situations. When God created man He established a relational system between himself and mankind designed to impart His values. God's values are still worthy to be embraced in our lives today. The single most important value we can transfer to our children is a loving commitment to God their creator. And second, ask yourself if you have the kind of relationship with God that you want to transfer to your children.

In other words, do we want our children to grow up to be like us—or different than us—in spiritual commitment, consistency, and character? Remember that we will only transfer those things that we possess. If we do not possess a vibrant, personal relationship with the Lord, we should make some changes to assure that we transfer the proper spiritual understanding and experiences to our children.

We must examine who we are in an honest way before we can concentrate on who we want our children to become. We must ask

> *Your children are influenced more by the life you model for them than by what you say, your good intentions, or any other factor of influence.*

ourselves: does our example conflict with or establish the proper model for our children to copy? Only when we are a positive example to them of what we are trying to transfer into their lives will they understand and apply what we have to say.

In recognizing the importance of this concept, we are actually finding one of the keys to successful parenting, which is a truth associated with principle of transference: our children are influenced more by the life we model for them than by what we say, our good intentions, or any other factor of influence. Therefore, the first consideration in any endeavor to "shape" our children is to create a standard—a positive example fashioned from our own lives to serve as the reference point and pattern for them to follow.

We must be shaped first. Only then can we deal with the secondary, but all-important question of how to choose the best methods for transferring the convictions and practices of our lives to our children in a proactive and effective manner. Hopefully, as you have read this section you have done a self review and as a result you are now ready to consider the godliness of your children.

Four Specific Times to Transfer Godliness

Long ago, my wife, Jan, and I individually committed to a personal, vibrant relationship with God. Our decision served as spiritual "insulation" from a lifeless practice of religious obligations, bland ceremonies, and pious procedures. At the same time, we committed to an all out effort to transfer our vibrant, personal, and active relationship with the Lord to our children. The question was: *How do we accomplish this?*

Jan and I had individually established personal quiet time dedicated to Bible study and prayer early in our lives. Our effort to establish this in our family proved difficult. Our children's ages varied so widely that it was hard to keep everyone's attention. Soon, the time became a boring obligation that everyone dreaded, defeating the purpose! The results were consistently disappointing.

But out of our disappointment, we discovered a better way. The book of Deuteronomy tells of a training method that is practical, powerful, and relationally dynamic. It is the extreme opposite of—and a welcome relief from—a dry, religious program. God's instruction for parents came from Moses with these words:

> *"And these words which I command you today shall be in your heart. 'You shall teach them diligently to your children, and shall talk of them when you sit in your house, when you walk by the way, when you lie down, and when you rise up." (Deuteronomy 6:6-7)*

God tells us that we are to train our children throughout the day as natural opportunities arise. There are four specific times mentioned:

1. When we "sit in our house," or as we enjoy home life;
2. When we "walk by the way," which today translates "to travel by car, plane, etc.;"
3. When we "lie down," or get ready for bed; and
4. When we "rise up," or as we prepare to start the day.

It is a lifestyle of "seizing the moment" as it arises throughout the day. From this viewpoint, daily circumstances become potential classrooms for teaching children to apply faith and other principles of godliness. This method is dynamic, practical, and personal. It tailors the training to their personality and experiences. More importantly, it is the only method I found that truly produced spiritual vibrancy in my children.

When I grew up, my family did not have devotions. We talked about God and we regularly attended church, but there were no family devotions. My understanding and training about God came from church. When I was 13, I went through communicance class so that I could join the church. It was dull, boring, and religious—it was lifeless! Through this experience I developed the idea that God is something important that we make a part of our life on Sunday, but He has little practical benefit or affect the other days of the week. My perception was based on my experience at home and in the church.

However, when I met Jesus in a personal way, I realized the concept of God that was formed by this experience was not right. I definitely did not want to transfer that false concept to my children, and I didn't want them to have that perception to overcome as they pursued and developed a relationship with God. It is this type of false perception that creates religious experiences, but not dynamic followers of Jesus Christ.

I am not against family devotions; if they produce good results for your family, use them. When they no longer produce the results you want, look for other creative ways to impart God's love and relationship to your children. Regardless of your method, here are

With kids, if you say it, you better mean it, and more importantly, you better be doing it.

several guidelines to help you make the transfer a success.

Guideline #1: *Walk the walk... don't simply talk the talk*

Children possess a wonderful ability to see through deception and pretense. With kids, if you say it, you better mean it, and more importantly, you better be doing it. For instance, if we as parents do not set the example by carving time for God out of our busy day, how can we advise our children how to do so when they ask us how to find time for God amidst all the pressures of their life—time with friends, school work, sports, and sleep? Our solution will carry no authority if we have not first solved this dilemma for ourselves. We must lead by example or the transfer will fail! Instruction, as the saying goes, is more caught than taught.

I talked with a father who was concerned and frustrated by his son's inability to control his temper. It was most notable when he competed in sporting events. His son would vent his frustration with demonstrations of anger at himself, on other players, his coach, the refs, and sometimes the fans. This young man was a polite and pleasant person to be around until he became frustrated by his performance in competition or he was upset by the injustice of call that did not go his way in a sporting event. Although his father was diligent to correct his son's outbursts, his correction seemed to have no lasting ability to change his son's behavior. As we talked, I agreed with his corrective response to his son's behavior and was puzzled by the lack of effectiveness until I played basketball with the father in a pick up game. His behavior was the same as his son's during the heat of competition. Then I understood why his correction was not working with his son. His own behavior was a stronger influence

A wise parent uses discernment to evaluate the teaching opportunity of the moment, and uses it to its fullest advantage.

than words of correction he had been giving his son. We cannot expect our children to do what we say if we are not able to do it ourselves. Our instruction just will not transfer.

Guideline #2: *Never waste an opportunity*

Teaching opportunities usually have two things in common: they are unexpected and inconvenient. When they come, we must take advantage of them because they may never be recreated.

Bedtime is a prime teaching time for young children. They seem to be most talkative and inquisitive just before going to bed. When this happened with my children, it was tempting to label their behavior as a charade, an attempt to milk the most out of the time so that they could put off going to sleep. A wise parent, however, uses discernment to evaluate the teaching opportunity of the moment, and uses it to its fullest advantage.

My dad looked for teaching moments throughout the day. At what seemed to be the strangest times, he would do something like this: as my family enjoyed causal conversation during dinner, my dad would out of the blue turn to one of my sisters or to me and say: "Do you know that I love your mother?"

My immediate thought was, "Uh oh, here it comes. Dad's on his soapbox again."

When he asked this, my sisters and I knew he was addressing all of us. "Yes dad," we would say in unison.

"Do you know that she was here before you?"

"Yes, Dad."

He would make eye contact with each one of us. "Do you know that she is going to be here after you're grown and gone?"

Our chorus was labored and weary now: "Yes, Dad."

"So don't try to get between your mom and me," he would say.

The final "yes, Dad" would finish the dialog and we would move on to another subject. It was painless and somewhat corny, but it etched an important value of his into our lives.

Good teachers sometimes resort to corny methods to impart a principle. As a child, you may have been turned off or even embarrassed by a "corny" lesson, yet later you retrieve the important principle or concept. What adult did not learn the alphabet by singing the corny little ditty "A-B-C-D-E-F-G..." as a child, only to recall it under his breath years later in a tense moment of game competition as he attempted to beat the clock and put a list of objects in alphabetic order?

The method might have been "corny," but the truth of the lesson stuck. In his "corniness", my dad taught us about his commitment to our mom and to their marriage. He declared their unity, along with establishing the reality that his relationship with her had priority in our family. He also exposed our tendency as children to manipulate by playing one parent against the other. So we knew that his relationship with her was a priority, and we never even tried to get between them to manipulate them.

In word and deed, my father imparted important values. He wanted his children to understand and adopt his pattern of priority, commitment, and unity as it relates to marriage. He was a wise teacher who knew that he must teach and enforce his values to his children at every opportunity. He knew that simply yelling at his children when they did something wrong, or teaching them only during times of discipline or crisis would not work.

If my dad had only attempted to teach us his values at a time when he was correcting our wrong behavior his efforts would have failed. This is where many fathers make a mistake. The primary time for training and imparting values is not while administering correction or at the point of frustration. We *reinforce* our values through correction, but we *impart* our values most effectively by seizing teachable moments as they arise in circumstances throughout the day. Therefore, influential fathering is a full-time responsibility, which requires the wise use of every opportunity and situation as a backdrop to illustrate and impart godly values and character.

Guideline #3: *Be consistent in your behavior and modeling of your values*

Nothing is more confusing for a child than inconsistently applied instruction. Parents must remember that a child thinks in concrete terms, and does not understand relative or abstract concepts. Thus, a child cannot make sense out of a parent who verbally stresses the importance of going to church, yet who attends one week and misses three.

To be influential fathers, we must make some tough decisions and commitments: Is telling the truth always the right thing to do, unless it's to a traffic cop or the I.R.S.? Is wholesome language important all the time, or only when the preacher is around? Do

> *...a parent must make sure his behavior is consistent with the values represented by his decisions, or his influence as a parent will be diminished and his values won't transfer.*

adults and children have the same moral parameters, or do adults have the right to selectively exclude certain standards?

Jan and I made a moral decision early in our life against drinking alcohol for reasons I more fully explain in Chapter 15. We of course understand that not every Christian will reach the same conclusion that we did, but we discussed our values regarding alcohol and the reasons behind it with each of our children as they reached their teen years. Our motive was to help them decide their position on this for their own life.

We all will make many moral decisions throughout our life affecting our behavior. While each person needs to make moral decisions for their own life, once those decisions have been made, a parent must make sure their behavior is consistent with the values represented by their decisions or their influence as a parent is diminished and their values won't transfer.

My dad was a smoker much to the concern of my mom and each of us kids. We were concerned for health reasons and were thrilled when he stopped smoking at 60 years old. As a child, I suffered from asthma and often my dad would tell me, "I smoke, but you shouldn't because you have asthma." As if his concern for my health was more important than our concern for his health. Once again the principle of transference comes into play. In this instance my dad failed to realize that his behavior had to be consistent with the value he held for it to transfer. Just having a conversation about his fatherly concern would not transfer the value for health he was trying to impart! My dad's input did not influence my decision on smoking because he was talking to me about a value he did not model in his own behavior.

Jan and I have been careful to watch for and eliminate inconsistent behavior in our lives as we point them out in our children's lives. One of these inconsistent "value" situations came up the summer after our eldest son, Todd, had graduated from high school. He had landed a job in the pro shop of a local golf course. One weekend, the golf course was host to a big tournament and one of the largest sponsors was the area beer distributor. On the final night of the tournament, Todd brought home a souvenir: a large, plastic beer bottle that had served as a tee marker for the tournament.

He presented it to Jan and I with fanfare, his face flush with excitement. "Isn't it cool?!" he exclaimed.

"Yeah," we said in unison, our enthusiasm noticeably less than his. Jan and I knew the bottle could not stay. It was inconsistent with our values, and we knew that somehow we must make it clear to Todd and our other children that graduation from high school did not exempt anyone from the standards of our home.

Jan and I talked about how to do this, pondering it for the next day or so. At the dinner table the next night, with Todd at work, our conversation turned to his newly acquired souvenir. "Isn't Todd's beer bottle cool?" blurted Lindsay, our youngest daughter. Her reaction confirmed what I already knew; something had to be done.

During Todd's high school years, he and I had talked a number of times about alcohol and drinking. I had thoroughly explained my position and the Biblical parameters for alcohol use. Our discussions had resulted in his decision to adopt my values as his own. He determined not to drink so that his life could have the greatest influence for God.

When he got home from work that night, I followed him up to his room.

"Todd," I said, in a calm voice, "I want to talk to you about your beer bottle."

His posture immediately turned defensive; he knew this conversation was coming. "Fine. Fine." he said. "I will take it out and throw it away."

"No, I am not asking you to do that," I said. My response stopped him dead in his tracks. "No," I said, "I want you to defend it."

There was a moment of silence and then he said, "What do you mean?"

"Well," I said, "have you changed your mind about drinking, and the importance of your influence on others?"

He looked at the beer bottle, then at me. "No," he said slowly.

I reminded him that in a few months he would be away at college—and in his dorm and fraternity, there would be guys who drank. I told him that if he wanted to be an influence on people around him, he must live consistently with his value's, and that when guys in the dorm dropped by his room and saw an item like the souvenir beer bottle, they would assume that he drank, too. And when he talked about God, the guys in the dorm could conclude that his relationship with the Lord was simply an intellectual, religious, or moral concept rather than a vibrant, personal, interactive, love-relationship. Our association with people, places, and things, I said, determines our influence on others, more than what we say.

A knock on the door momentarily paused our conversation. Lindsay, who was five at the time, poked her head in to remind me that she was ready for me to pray with her and tuck her into bed. Suddenly, her eyes caught the souvenir beer bottle and her face lit up. "Hey Todd," she exclaimed, "I think your beer bottle is really cool!"

When she had shut the door, I looked at Todd and said, "I rest my case. In one night, your association with this bottle has sent a message. Is it the message you want to send? Is this the kind of influence you want to have on the people around you?"

"No," he said.

I reminded him that he could not say it wasn't cool to drink, if at the same time, he represented that it was cool to have a souvenir beer bottle. The inconsistency will confuse the people around you, I told him.

I left the room to pray with Lindsay and to allow Todd some time to think about our conversation. I did not ask him to remove his souvenir, because the issue was not his souvenir, it was the message of inconsistency it represented and the shadow it placed on his influence to others, in this case his siblings. That night, he hauled his souvenir to the trash. He had realized that, even if it was "really cool," it was an object inconsistent with his values.

We must realize in evaluating actions or behavior that the issue at hand is not always the "real" issue needing to be addressed. A father came to me concerned about the appearance of his teenage son, who had recently gone out and had his ear pierced and was talking about getting a tattoo. He wanted to know how he should deal with his son on this issue.

First I questioned this father about his personal life and what it represents. Reminding him that it is impossible to transfer something we do not possess for our self. I told him that he needed to make sure that what his life represented was consistent with the value he wanted to reinforce in his son. As I discussed with this father his own life and the values he held, the discussion enabled us

You build a platform to teach and transfer your values to your children through making sure your actions are consistent with the values that you hold and seek to transfer.

to discover and clarify why he was concerned about his son's earring.

In his understanding an earring was an outward sign of rebellion or defiance. He did not want his son identified by such a stereotype even if it was stylish within his age group. Once we identified the underlying value that formed the basis for concern, it gave the father a platform for discussing his concern with his son. As it turned out, when he approached his son to discuss the issue, he agreed to allow his son to keep a modest earring acknowledging that it might not have to indicate rebellion or defiance. His son heard his dad's concern about what his actions could indicate to others and decided not to get a tattoo.

Of course, your issues may be different than the ones I am describing, they are different with each child, they may even be more serious than the ones presented here, but I assure you the principles for influencing your children toward godliness will work even though the issues differ. Uncover the value represented by your

You must present God in a
positive light in
everything you say and do.

concern, check to make sure your own actions are consistent with the value you are seeking to transfer or reinforce in your child, and present your concerns in a loving and relational way.

We build a platform to teach and transfer our values to our children through making sure our actions are consistent with the values that we hold and seek to transfer.

Guideline #4: *Make it fun to focus on God*

I am completely convinced that God is into fun. The Bible clearly tells us that He takes great pleasure in our joy and celebration before Him. *"The Lord your God in your midst, The Mighty One, will save;"* the Scripture says, *"He will rejoice over you with gladness...He will rejoice over you with singing."* (Zephaniah 3:17)

Of course, we must also teach our children reverence for God. Most importantly, we must present God in a positive light in everything we say and do.

Until our children reached their teen years, I would sing and pray with them before bedtime. On many evenings, I would gather all four of my kids in a bedroom, and with my guitar in hand, I would lead them in singing praise to God. The kids had great fun dancing, jumping on the bed, and sometimes running down the hall. Why not, I thought, we're celebrating here. Their fun-loving excitement filled me with joy. I can only imagine how pleasing it must have been to God.

To keep them focused on God, I required them to sing as they celebrated. Jan required that we kept the craziness to a dull roar.

In our home, we successfully imparted our values to our children in a positive atmosphere of fun and celebration. Today, all of our children are grown. All—without exception—have a deeply committed personal relationship with Christ. All—without exception—have accepted the values that we sought to transfer.

Jan and I do not have special abilities that have guaranteed the successful transfer of our values to our children. Everyone can do what we have done. The requirement is that each of us live what we teach, and teach it in a way that our children can understand and accept.

A Concluding Thought

"Which is the greatest commandment in the law?" a lawyer asked Jesus. Jesus said to him: *"You shall love the LORD your God with all your heart, with all your soul, and with all your mind."* (Matthew 22:36)

In other words, Jesus said to love God with everything that you are—love Him with your whole being. Translating that love to our children requires a positive, personal example. It also requires us to create and maintain an atmosphere of consistent instruction and a positive, love-centered accountability for each member of the family.

Through our discussion in this chapter you may have realized that you are lacking in your example to your children. You may have been convicted concerning some inconsistency in your behavior or values, or maybe your commitment to God has become religious or boring. God is a God of grace and will accept your response to Him. Isaiah 1:18 says:

> *"Come now and let us reason together, says the LORD, Though your sins are like scarlet, They shall be as white as snow; Though they are red like crimson, They shall be as wool. If you are willing and obedient, you shall eat of the good of the land."*

Don't delay. Make the appropriate changes today. Walking the walk, never wasting an opportunity, being consistent, and making it fun to focus on God will help you form an effective plan. As you do this, you will ensure that your values will transfer to your children, and as God promised in Isaiah, you and your family will "eat of the good of the land."

CHAPTER 4

Developing a Healthy Fear
of God in Your Children

*The correct understanding of the fear
of God has at its foundation
the confidence of God's approving
love and affection.
Most people, however, do not associate the
fear of God with these terms.*

To many people, the fear of God is a negative concept. He is often thought of as a menacing figure that scrutinizes our every deed with fervor, eagerly waiting for us to mess up so He can stir our lives with His spoon full of wrath. This belief is reflected in a response like this: "I don't go to church, and I know someday I'll pay the price for it."

The perception is that God is out to teach us to do what He says or be prepared to pay the price. The irony is that although this thinking dominates western culture, it has had little influence on shaping behavior. Eighty-six percent of Americans profess to believe in God, and 79% profess to believe in a Judgment Day before God. Yet only 46% say they attend church regularly, and only 16% of Americans say they read the Bible on a consistent basis![4]

The church parallels society in almost every measurable statistic: divorce, teen pregnancy, abortion, bankruptcy, etc. Fearing God's wrath has not had any real effect on the behavior patterns of those who claim to follow God. Why is that? Simply stated, it is because the fear of retribution does not change a heart; only love can accomplish that!

Why do some children avoid developing a pattern of bad behavior, and others are drawn to it like a magnet? I believe the primary factor that determines a child's avoidance or attraction to these activities is a loving respect for his parents, a desire to make them proud. When an attitude of love and respect toward his parents does not shadow his decision making process, a control mechanism intended to guide proper behavior is missing, too. When the control mechanism is missing it opens the door to foolish behavior, influenced by the pressure of friends or the whim of the moment. The results can be tragic. Pranks and even more sinister deeds, such as illegal or immoral acts, are waiting to trap our children in a moment of foolish indiscretion.

During my high school years, I avoided many pitfalls by using this simple method of evaluation: *If I get caught, what will my parents think?* My love and respect for my parents, coupled with my desire to represent them in my behavior were governing factors that brought cautious consideration before participating in any activity.

My children have used this same method to evaluate their participation in activities. In essence, this thinking represents the

> *Love and respect for my parents were governing factors that brought cautious consideration before participating in any activity.*

kind of fear that children should have for their parents—a fear of disappointing them, a fear of not properly representing them and their values. Children should never fear rejection nor should we use the fear of rejection to motivate their behavior. Correction is necessary, but rejection is damaging to our children.

While I love and respect my mom, it was my dad who cast the largest shadow over my consideration. The reason is that a dad is the doorkeeper of his home. What he allows into the home will be tolerated; what he resists will be systematically rooted out.

I once counseled a man named Ben, who was in a business that demanded he spend a lot of his time away from home. He thought the best way he could influence his son was to make their home the gathering point for his son's circle of friends. In order to ensure their home was a gathering place for the teenagers, he raised no standard for their behavior. He felt it might seem judgmental if he monitored their activities around his house. It might even drive them away! It worked, his home became a gathering place for the teenagers.

However without a standard for acceptable behavior that was communicated and enforced, his home attracted the rebellious and troubled teens in his son's school. The influence of these teens began to affect the behavior of his son, so he came to me and asked what he should do. I encouraged him to set a standard for behavior consistent with the values he modeled in his own life. To be kind and gracious in his enforcement of the standard but to make unwelcome any teen that was unwilling to abide by the standard he raised.

Ben could not do what I suggested because he thought it judged the kids and would drive them away along with his son. He was grieved when his son rebelled against him and the things he and his wife believed. But he never did realize his son's behavior was the result of his failure to be the doorkeeper of his home.

Defining the Fear of God

We cannot fully understand the fear of God and its shaping influence on behavior apart from this kind of relationship with our fathers. In its essence, the fear of God is demonstrated through attitudes and actions of reverent respect.

My father influenced our family by his character and guidance, not by intimidation. I wanted to please him because I loved and respected him. My desire to please him created a fear of disappointing him. My respect for my father and the corresponding desire to please him were never the result of fearing rejection.

Children develop a framework for understanding God through the relationship that they have with their parents, especially the relationship with their father. If he is dominating, harsh, and controlling, then in his child's mind, God is also dominating, harsh, and controlling.

I have known Dave for twenty years. He is a good father with a successful career and has been consistent in his love and service to God, but he has always struggled to believe that God really loves him, and he finds it almost impossible that he could do anything that would please God. I have prayed with him many times and through counseling shared passages of Scripture to assure him that God loved him, showing him that the Bible is very clear that God accepts us just as we are, and He actually rejoices over us with singing (Zephaniah 3:17). Although that input brought momentary comfort, it didn't stay with him for long. Growing up, Dave's dad was harsh and punitive in the way he related to him. As long as Dave pleased his dad, his dad was kind and accepting of him, but if he ever messed up, he experienced his dad's wrath and rejection.

Although Dave is doing better today, it has been years of struggle to separate his image of God's love and acceptance from the pattern of love, acceptance, and rejection modeled by his dad.

As I discussed in Chapter 2, a child's perception of God is so influenced by his relationship with his father that it is not easily changed even with Biblical references of truth that reveal the true nature of God's love as different than what they experienced from their father.

When understood, this truth has a profound effect on the way a father relates to his children. His actions and reactions build the children's framework for understanding God, especially in the children's primary years. He is the image of "God" that his young children see and that his older children relate to.

Understanding the Fear of God

...the fear of God translates into a reverent respect that is motivated by heartfelt love. It produces a desire to please God through attitudes and actions.

The foundation for a correct understanding of the fear of God is the personal confidence we have of God's approving love and affection. Most people, however, do not associate the fear of God with these terms. But when correctly understood and applied, the fear of God translates into a reverent respect that is motivated by heartfelt love. It produces a desire to please God through attitudes and actions. When behavior has missed the mark, it is the loving respect we have for God that becomes the catalyst that produces heartfelt remorse. How is this type of response to God learned, if not from the relational interaction between a father and his children?

An incident from my high school years affords an example. On a Friday night, my friends and I drove into the parking lot of an arch rival school across town to attend a basketball game. Anticipating victory, we stepped out of the car with youthful arrogance and walked toward the gym. From across the parking lot, someone yelled obscenities at us. We spun on our heels, our adrenaline pumping. In seconds, we were in a fight—with me at the center.

A police officer arrived instantly, stopped the brawl, and escorted me and my opponent—the main fighters—to the gym. I had never been a troublemaker before, so I think it surprised my high school principal to see me coming into the gym under police escort. He listened as the cop related all the details of the incident, then he suspended me on the spot, pending a conversation with my father. He immediately sent me home from the game. My night was ruined.

My mom was surprised to see me arrive home early. After I told her what had happened she told me, "You'll need to tell your dad when he gets home."

Dad was at a business meeting, and not expected home until midnight. I suggested that since I was really tired, and she was going to be up anyway, she could tell him for me. That idea didn't fly.

It was the longest wait of my life.

Although I was confident of his love, my heart sank as I thought of his disappointment. I had let him down. I knew that my actions did not represent him or his values. It was not his punishment or retribution that I feared. It was the anticipation of his disappointment for failing to represent his values in my conduct that weighed so heavily on my thoughts.

To this day, I vividly remember my feelings of that night: our cockiness on the way to the game, the machismo and adrenaline rush of the fight, and finally, the anxious anticipation of my dad's response.

When he came home, I told him everything, finishing with the suspension, which would continue, I told him, until he talked to the principal. I had disappointed myself by my actions, and I knew I had disappointed him. Without excusing my behavior, my dad affirmed his love for me and clearly communicated his expectation that this type of behavior should not happen again. I assured him it would not. I was regretful, and he knew it.

On Monday, I waited in the secretary's office as my dad talked with the principal. After what seemed like an eternity, my dad and the principal emerged with smiles and handshakes. I returned to class never to repeat that kind of thing again.

Respect for my dad continues to influence my life to this day. It is the essence of the "fear" I had of him, and it has formed the foundation for my "fear" of God. My dad's standards, which he established, modeled, and enforced in our home, continue to produce profound personal benefits for me. His actions built a bridge of understanding that has enabled me to receive God's loving acceptance even when I fail. Also, it showed me the importance of my behavior and how it reflects, either positively or negatively, on him.

Jeff was a young man that lived in our neighborhood. His parents were good neighbors, good parents, and Jeff's dad was a leader in their church. But, Jeff's dad was busy with work and social responsibilities and expected his son not to cause him problems.

When Jeff was in elementary school he had some discipline problems and his dad was very upset with both the school and Jeff. Unfortunately, he was more concerned with the inconvenience this caused him than with the pattern it indicated in Jeff's behavior. So he yelled at his son, verbally belittling him all the way from the car to the house. Jeff's dad also made sure that all the neighbors knew he was upset by his son's behavior. However, there was no real attention to his son's behavior problem at the school, just the clear message to his son that if he wanted to avoid his wrath, he'd better not inconvenience his father.

As Jeff grew into his teens he became adept at slick explanations for his increasingly bizarre behavior so that his dad was appeased and not inconvenienced. The school officials and the neighbors were aware of his son's escalating behavior problems, but his dad did not have to get involved, so to him Jeff was okay.

When Jeff's behavior resulted in problems with the local police and a reputation among friends and neighbors as being mean and vindictive, his dad's reputation was affected. No longer was it an issue of inconvenience, now it was an issue of reputation that extended from Jeff to his dad and affected his work and influence in the community—not to mention the problems that Jeff faced cleaning up his damaged reputation.

Jeff's behavior was not governed by loving respect for his parents or by a desire to represent them in the way he acted. Jeff's dad did nothing to change that and in essence approved his behavior by his passive response. In so doing, the dad sabotaged the mechanism that God intended to help govern and guide his son in proper behavior; therefore, Jeff made no connection between his behavior, the reputation it produced, and the negative reflection it cast on his mom and dad.

The Connection Between Fearing Our Fathers and Fearing God

A child's decision to honor his parents is developed by a father who raises and then enforces a standard through positive interaction and correction of his children.

The primary responsibility of a father is to establish, model, and enforce a standard for behavior in his family. While fulfilling this responsibility, he must also hold his children accountable for their behavior, giving them a pattern to follow, and graciously correcting them when their behavior doesn't conform to the pattern. A desire to honor and please will not be formed in our children without this important work guided by their father. When a desire to honor and please exists in a child toward his father, it is easily developed and transferred into the child's relationship with God. When there is not an attitude of respectful honor in children for their father—and mother—a reverent respect for God will not develop either.

The Bible instructs children to honor their parents. Ephesians 6 gives us a command with a promise, *"Children, obey your parents in the Lord, for this is right...that it may be well with you and you may live long on the earth."* A child's decision to honor his parents is developed by a father who raises and then enforces a standard through positive interaction and correction of his children.

Some fathers confuse dependence with honor. They mistake the respectful requests from their children for money, clothes, or other wants for an attitude of honor. When in reality their children's response is polite, maybe even manipulative, motivated by their desire for a selfish benefit.

The honor we are looking to produce in our children flows from a heart of love, not a manipulative desire to get a benefit or avoid punishment. Honor cannot be expressed in words only, but must be reflected in behavior.

Many Christians today struggle with erratic patterns of behavior, never really finding the inner-discipline to live and act correctly. Rick was a single young man in our church. He struggled with a sexual sin that constantly tempted him to do what he knew was wrong.

When he would give in to the temptation, he was remorseful and came quickly to confess his wrong behavior—often with great emotion. The confession coupled with his demonstration of remorse eased his conscience, which is a good fruit produced by repentance.

Rick's knowledge of God and the Bible produced the right words, coupled with tears of remorse; however it had no real or lasting effect on his behavior. As I discussed this pattern of behavior with him, I discovered that he had no relationship with his dad. His mom and dad were divorced, and his dad had left them when Rick was a young boy. He had no honor or respect for his father or his father's values. He had no fear represented in reverent respect for his father because he had never been a part of his life. As a result, Rick had no fear of God that is represented in honoring behavior that seeks to reflect his father's character and values.

Rick's remorse for wrong behavior was not strong enough to lead him to actions that he knew were right. He lacked the mechanism for guiding his behavior and he had no concept of pleasing or honoring his father, or God, through the conduct of his life.

The fear of God that is represented by the desire to honor and please Him is created through the relationship between a father and his children. Words alone do not demonstrate the presence of reverent respect. The words must be reflected in behavior consistent with the values imparted from their father. Until this relational dynamic exists between a father and his children, God's mechanism to motivate appropriate behavior will not operate properly in their lives. God's corrective action is to assure that our words and actions are consistent with His values:

> "...we have had human fathers who corrected us...For they indeed for a few days chastened us as seemed best to them, but He for our profit, that we may be partakers of His holiness." (Hebrews 12:9-10)

In other words, the purpose of God's correction is to protect us from the damage of sin, so that we might enjoy the long-term benefits of His Holy Spirit in our lives— benefits such as love, joy, peace, longsuffering, kindness, and more (Galatians 5:22). Just believing and speaking God's standard does not produce behavior that represents Him. God disciplines, corrects, and influences His children, consistently revealing His character by never violating the individual's freedom of choice and by never bringing correction through threat or intimidation.

Jesus did not force His disciples to follow by threat or intimidation. They followed Him by choice because they understood His character and embraced His standard of values as their own.

> "From that time many of His disciples went back and walked with Him no more. Then Jesus said to the twelve,

'Do you also want to go away?' But Simon Peter answered Him: 'Lord, to whom shall we go? You have the words of eternal life. Also we have come to believe and know that You are the Christ, the Son of the living God.' " (John 6:66-69)

A relationship that threatens punitive action or rejection for wrong behavior does not create the proper motivation for behavior in you or in your children.

Simon Peter recognized that Jesus knew the right way, and he chose to follow Him! He stayed with Jesus because he had come to love and respect Him, and he knew there was no one like Him. Peter was not motivated to follow God by fear that some catastrophe would befall him if he went his own way! He responded with love to Jesus because of the character and the standard for living he saw in Him. A relationship that threatens punitive action or rejection for wrong behavior does not create the proper motivation for behavior in us or in our children.

Introducing God to our children as a Person who reacts with punitive force is the wrong method for correcting behavior. It reflects a distorted image of God and produces behavior based on a religious system of legalism and performance. Telling our children that God is mad at them for certain behavior and warning them of impending judgment is also not effective in changing or controlling their behavior. Above all, it is a misrepresentation of God's disposition toward us.

To be sure, those who reject God while on earth should fear the punishment reserved for the final judgment. We need to inform our children of this truth. However, they must know that "Judgment Day" fear is reserved for the lost, who on that day will experience first an overwhelming regret for ignoring God's loving offer of forgiveness. It will be compounded by a remorseful agreement with His judgment of their personal sin, and finally, the dawning horror of eternal separation from Him. God desires from His children a relationship of reverent respect that is reflected in attitude and actions, generated from a heart that loves Him and sincerely seeks to please Him.

How do we produce this in our children? We begin by transferring our values through a clearly defined standard for behavior.

Define and Communicate Your Standard

God defined and communicated His values for humanity in the Ten Commandments. Yet God's love for us is not dependent upon our successful fulfillment of His laws, a truth for which we should be exceedingly grateful. Rather, His law serves to provide us a model; a standard for behavior that properly reflects His character while revealing our need for Him.

Fathers fail to define a standard for one primary reason: *we are selfish*. We do not want to be accountable for our behavior.

If there is no standard, the effort to train and shape your children will fail.

Common excuses go something like this: "I must remain open-minded" or "standards stifle creativity." In reality, these excuses only hide an independent unwillingness to be accountable.

Failure to define a standard leaves us with nothing to communicate and enforce within our families. Without a standard, a mishmash of rules are created and enforced inconsistently as circumstances require or as is convenient to the mood of the moment. The inconsistent non-standard produces the equivalent of a moving target of values for our children to try and aim for. Both frustrating and confusing, it produces poor results—in target practice and in child development. If there is no standard, the effort to train and shape our children will fail.

Jim and Sue came to my office to discuss Sue's frustration with Jim and the problem it was producing with their children. It seems that Jim is a happy go lucky guy—the life of any party. Sue enjoys and appreciates that about him, but along with his easy-going, fun-loving nature comes a resistance to define anything by absolutes.

As I questioned him I found that he could not absolutely say it was wrong to steal, or to murder, or to cheat. To him the situation determined what was appropriate. Only when I would describe the situation could he tell me if the behavior was wrong. Without knowing the situation, he was unwilling to label most any behavior as wrong. This was the source of conflict and concern for Sue.

They could have no rules for their children because each situation determined what was right or wrong. It might or might not be wrong for one of the children to come in past curfew. It just depended on the situation. Jim did not want to set any general curfew; he wanted to set it based on each event. But it went further than defining a general time the children needed to be home at night. It covered almost every area of their life.

Was it wrong to disobey the school administration? Was it wrong to break the law? To Jim it all depended on the circumstances. I asked Jim if he had values that governed his life. He was firmly convinced he had values, but as we talked he admitted he could not define his values apart from specific situations. Since Jim could not define his values apart from specific situations, Sue and Jim had no values to communicate to their children apart from specific situations. They could not impart values for behavior and living until after a situation developed and because details would change from situation to situation, what was wrong in one situation might be ok in another.

Sue agreed with me that this created a moving target for monitoring their children's behavior. She dealt first hand with the confusion and frustration her children felt without clearly defined values for behavior that were independent from situations or circumstances. If there is no defined standard our effort to train our children and transfer our values to them will fail.

Associating Performance with Acceptance

It is as dangerous to our children's welfare to associate love and acceptance with their performance, as it is to fail to define a

When parents establish and transfer a standard for behavior, they are defining boundaries, which provide security and protection.

standard. When the motive for good behavior is the fear of rejection, our children develop a performance concept of love rather than an acceptance concept of love. They learn that if they do right they will be accepted and loved, but if they do wrong, they will be rejected. Parents teach this concept of performance acceptance when they extend love and relationship based on their children's behavior or activities conforming to the expectations of their standard.

When parents establish and transfer a standard for behavior, they are defining boundaries represented by values for their children. The boundaries provide security and protection, and they are good, necessary, and beneficial for their development. However, a standard becomes a weapon of emotional and spiritual destruction when it is associated with love and acceptance of our children. Acceptance must remain on the basis of relationship—never to be based on performance.

I remind you that God does not love us in this way.

God's love is without conditions. He loves us even though He knows the worst about us. His blessings are conditional based upon our response, but His love is unconditional. It may seem like a paradox, to love and accept our children in spite of their foolish actions.

You might wonder how *acceptance* creates the reverent respect and the desire to please that is necessary to shape behavior. Acceptance is the reflection of love that is patient and kind, that believes all things, hopes all things, and endures all things (1 Corinthians 13). *Rejection* does not create acceptance of our values, an honor and respect, or a desire to please. These qualities are only created through proactive love. We do not have to perform to receive God's love and neither should our children have to perform to receive our love.

If we are going to represent God to our children and transfer to them a proper understanding of His love and care, our actions must be consistent with His nature. We must teach values and uphold a standard without attaching our acceptance to successful performance. God holds us to a standard by correcting us when we miss the mark. So, we must correct our children when they miss the mark in their actions. However, correction should not equate to rejection.

God has separated His love and acceptance of us from the standard He has established for our behavior; we must do the same for our children. He is imparting His values into our lives. And through His grace, He is loving us just as we are—imperfections and all. He loves us enough to impart His values by correcting us when we fail to meet His standard, without rejecting us for failed effort! That is true love, the concept we want to represent and transfer to our children.

When we enforce the standard through rigid demands, or associate acceptance of our children with their performance to the standard, we create an atmosphere for legalism. Legalism is the inflexible enforcement of a standard of rules tied to performance.

The much-publicized fall from ministry of Jimmy Swaggart in the late 1980's and early 1990's provides an example of this truth. Jimmy Swaggart is a gifted musician, songwriter, and preacher. He was the founder and leader of a dynamic worldwide ministry.

Leading up to his public embarrassment and removal from ministry (he was caught in a motel room with a prostitute), he could be seen preaching an unbending standard of holy and righteous living.

His preaching was passionate against immorality, adultery, and pornography. His rigid application of Biblical passages raised a standard for right living, but it also created an atmosphere for legalism and self-righteousness. Ultimately, the legalism that enforced the standard he raised, became a covering for his own unrighteous behavior—behavior that was contrary and inconsistent with the message he was preaching. His presentation of the standard was inflexible and offered no grace for failure to meet the standard.

Our parenting goal is not to raise and apply a standard of behavior that becomes a tool of destruction to our children. Paul and Sally are a couple who love God and serve Him with passion. They live a life of commitment to God and demonstrate a high standard for behavior based on the values they live and believe. However, their children are a mess. Their four children each have rejected the standard of their parents as they matured into their upper teens and early twenty's, each refusing to adopt their parents standard as their own.

Why? How does a committed couple that is passionate in their love and service for God fail to pass their love and values on to their children? The answer lies in the application and enforcement of their standard for behavior. Paul and Sally left no room for their children to grow into their service and passion for God. It was expected and demanded. It was legislated on them by Paul and Sally.

An attitude of resistance was labeled as rebellion. If their children's passion turned toward sports, dating, cars, clothes, or other teenage interests, their parents questioned their love for God. They also left no room for failure to achieve the standard even with diligent effort on their children's behalf. Over time the rigid application of their standard produced an angry rejection in all their children for Paul and Sally's standard. It brought disappointment and heartbreak to them along with a sense of failure as parents.

Paul and Sally's high standard and expectations of proper

behavior did not produce the response they desired in their children. Legalism perverts the proper fear of God, replacing it with a cheap substitute, not based on love and honor, but on performance and rules. Legalism is a harsh taskmaster that without exception produces rejection of the standard and rebellion to the rules being enforced.

Avoid the Two Extremes of Legalism

Legalism is acceptance with strings attached.

When legalism is present, it is commonly found in one of two dangerous extremes. The first extreme is to raise the standard, but have no method of enforcement. The father may have communicated his standards to his children, yet he has an unhealthy attitude that that allows his children to live below the standard because he feels no one can completely live up to the standard he has raised. In this situation, mercy overrules truth. The relationship is valued but the standard for measuring behavior is compromised; there is no accountability.

At the beginning of this chapter I told the story of Ben and his reaction to raising and enforcing a standard with his children. His

Only loving acceptance connected to a clearly defined standard will create the desire in your children to make you proud of their behavior.

focus was totally on the relationship he desired with his children. The relationship was highly valued in his eyes to the neglect of raising and enforcing a standard of behavior for his children.

The second extreme is to connect the standard to the relationship, which means: if you don't measure up, you lose the relationship. Paul and Sally always had one or more of their children in trouble for failing to live up to their standard. They were harsh and punitive in their punishment of their children. Isolating them from the family and removing privileges to drive home their disappointment with pain and rejection.

In this extreme, truth overrules mercy as value is placed on performance, and the quality of the relationship is compromised. When love and respect do not motivate our children to adopt our standard of behavior, something is wrong. Forcing the correct behavior by using a threat of rejection works for a short while, but it will not sustain a permanent lifestyle of proper behavior in our children. It ultimately produces resentment and destroys the relationship between parents and their children. Only loving acceptance connected to a clearly defined standard will create the desire in our children to make us proud of their behavior.

Concluding Thoughts

If you grew up with an abusive or dominant father, this chapter may have reminded you of painful memories. Based on your experience, it may be difficult for you to comprehend the idea of loving respect for your father as a motive for proper behavior and to embrace it as the basis of establishing a love and respect for God. It may be hard to see God in any other light than the light of your father's treatment of you. You may even struggle with abusive or dominant tendencies toward your children.

Even though your experience has not been good, understanding this concept is important to developing a healthy relationship with God and living a stable life pleasing to Him. Do you respect and honor your father? Do your children honor and respect you? Is there the kind of healthy respect we discussed in this chapter between you and your children? Do they have a loving desire to please you? Or do you relate to them by the fear of intimidation or abusive dominance? Do you accept or reject them based on their performance?

If you need to forgive your father for his failure or abuse imposed on your life, why not take a moment to offer up a prayer of forgiveness? Ask God to help you forgive your father and heal the hurts of your childhood. Ask Him to help you understand for yourself how to raise a standard for behavior without linking acceptance to performance. Ask God to help you train your children to honor and respect you in a healthy way so that they will live their adult life with honor and respect for God and His ways. He will answer your prayer and teach you His way.

CHAPTER 5
A Matter of Character

To accomplish truly great things with results that are lasting, our efforts must align with God's plans and His methods. God's work performed in God's way produces God's results. He is not impressed by results that have been produced using methods that are inconsistent with His nature.

During the presidency of Bill Clinton, the subject of character was a topic of heated debate. Many insisted that character didn't matter as long as the president was doing a good job. The populace seemed unwilling to judge individual character. Instead, the performance of the President was measured by the results he produced, rather than by the standards he upheld.

When results are the only measuring stick for individual achievement, character is excluded and a door is opened for dangerous, immoral, or unethical behavior to be accepted. But the Bible tells us in Proverbs chapter fourteen that *"righteousness exalts a nation, But sin is a reproach to any people."*

Character does not mean perfection. It does not establish authority for self-righteousness and intolerance. Instead, character relates to our standards of value. It forms the framework for the expression of our personalities and talents. It is the moral and ethical structure for our actions, the bedrock of our thinking, the basis for our treatment of people, and our response to circumstances. Left unchallenged or uncorrected, character flaws become strongholds of weakness that control the individual and cause pain to those closest to him.

Almost everyone has exaggerated circumstances as they retold a story to a friend or family members. However, when exaggeration becomes a pattern of communication it must be addressed. Exaggerations are lies in seed form. The step from an exaggeration to a deliberate manipulation of truth, which is what a lie is, is not a very big step. A pattern of lying reveals the character flaw of dishonesty.

Therefore, we must treat even small issues with serious-minded resolve. We cannot even allow bad attitudes to be tolerated or go unchallenged because attitudes generate thoughts, thoughts lead to actions, actions develop habits, habits form character, and character determines destiny!

Imagine beginning a long trip in a car with a flawed tire. The flawed tire may perform adequately on short drives around town, and may even go unnoticed for a number of miles at high speed. Yet the potential for disaster is always present. A blowout on the highway could result in severe injuries, even death. Those who have experienced this understand first-hand the seriousness of a minor flaw left unchecked.

Imagine being in business with a person who is dishonest and their character flaw shows up in pressure situations, when they are

> *...attitudes generate thoughts, thoughts lead to actions, actions develop habits, habits form character, and character determines destiny!*

threatened with loss, hurt, or rejection. In the face of this kind of pressure, they will do anything to avoid the personal pain. Let's presume, that in the natural growth of your business, a crisis will inevitably develop. Possibly one like this; your business becomes strapped for capital, and it looks like you and your partner are going to need to take less income out of the business in order to survive the crisis. Your partner is responsible for the business and accounting operations and in order to avoid the personal sacrifice associated with the cutback, he begins embezzling funds from the business. His character flaw has now affected the day-to-day conduct of your business. Under routine business it didn't show up, but under the pressure of an extreme business crisis, it is revealed. The potential devastation to you and your business is incalculable even to the point of threatening your very existence.

Character is what determines our responses to difficult situations that develop in our lives. When we speak of character, we speak of qualities like these: faithfulness, honesty, truthfulness, diligence, loyalty, bravery, generosity, patience, and the ability to receive correction. Even a cursory look at this list should make the significance of character apparent; it has an important influence on behavior and therefore on circumstances.

Which of us would want to enter into any important endeavor with someone of questionable character? Would you want to put your life on the line and depend upon someone who lacked character qualities? Every day we rely upon the character of people. We trust in the President of the United States as commander-in-chief to lead the military in defending our nation. We call upon police and law enforcement personnel to enforce the law and make our communities safe. We depend upon counter-terrorism units to thwart disasters, such as the one that brought down the World Trade Center on 9/11/01, not to mention the people who control our nuclear weapons systems, or the air traffic controllers and pilots who take us safely from one place to another. Almost everywhere we look, we depend upon the character and integrity of people around us to perform their jobs. We rely on character so much that it is often taken for granted until someone without character acts, and we are confronted with the destructive results.

Over years of giving pre-marriage counseling, I've found that one of the most important aspects of pre-marriage preparation is to identify and correct character flaws. When I am talking to a young couple I ask them for details about their life apart from the life they are developing with their fiancée. I ask them to tell me about their work experience. I ask them how many jobs they have held. Through the answers to these questions I am looking for signs that indicate a character weakness like laziness or slothful attitudes or behavior.

Craig and Rachel were a young pre-marriage couple I was counseling in preparation for their wedding day. As I was asking them questions to get to know them better, my questions served a secondary purpose. They were helping me to identify and uncover character weaknesses to address in our counseling.

As we talked Craig revealed the he had been at his current job almost a year. He commented to Rachel that was the longest time he had ever been at one job in his life. Craig was in his mid-twenties and his comment raised a flag that could be critical in the success of their marriage. Faithfulness, diligence, and a willingness to work hard are qualities that reflect character. They are also qualities that are critical for the long-term success of a marriage.

Early in my pastoral ministry I would have overlooked a comment like Craig's, failing to realize the connection. But after a few couples whose wedding ceremony I conducted went on to divorce, I began to make a connection, realizing that character issues impact all areas of life.

As I worked with Craig in counseling, I found he did have a character weakness that affected his employment. We worked to correct and identify attitudes of laziness and attitudes that made him unreliable as an employee. Craig worked hard to change behavior and thinking that not only helped him to become a better employee—but also prepared him to succeed in marriage.

I can't think of a couple I have encountered through my pastoral ministry that had an expectation that their partner would be unfaithful or fail to fulfill their responsibilities in the marriage. Despite our best efforts we all fall short of perfection but some people fail at critical points of character weakness whether in marriage, friendship, or on the job. Critical failure based on character is devastating. So, you ask, is character really that important? Absolutely!

On an individual level, regardless of our talent, we cannot develop into the persons God desires or fulfill His destiny for our lives apart from our character. It is true that individuals lacking character have accomplished noteworthy deeds, if only measured by results like: the power of their influence, their net worth or financial influence, even their physical size. Eventually though, deficiency in character exacts its price—whether in family relations, personal health, reputation, finances, or some other area.

President Clinton is an example of how a person can accomplish noteworthy deeds without character. To become president of the United States is a noteworthy accomplishment. Questions related to character were constant during his presidency, spanning his whole political career. We know he did not tell the truth to the American people or to the grand jury investigating his relationship with Monica Lewinsky. The results of his unfaithfulness and inability to tell the truth were millions of dollars of legal bills, embarrassment to his wife and daughter, a strain on his marriage, and a vote for impeachment by the United States Senate. Only time will reveal the full extent of the damage done as a result of his weakness in character.

Any achievement produced without character is temporary; any effort solely focused on results will not satisfy especially when measured by God in the light of eternity.

To accomplish truly great things with results that are lasting, our efforts must align with God's plans and His methods. *God's work performed in God's way produces God's results.* He is not impressed by results that have been produced using methods that are inconsistent with His nature.

Human character was intended to be a direct reflection of the nature of God. He is the essence of true character; everything good, wholesome, and pure began in Him. It does not matter what our motive is, or if the result is for a good cause. When we lie, cheat, or steal to get a desired result, He is not impressed. In God's system, the end never justifies the means.

Just as parents know that their children's behavior is a reflection on them, God also knows that if we claim to be His followers, our behavior is a reflection on Him. Therefore, He expects our lives to be lived in a way that represents and reflects His character. Through the partnership established between God and parents, character is emphasized and developed. In his role as the leader of his family, it becomes a father's responsibility to represent and reinforce the qualities of God's character in his children.

How Is Character Developed?

The New Testament book of James gives us an understanding of God's method of character development. The pattern is laid out in the first chapter:

> *"My brethren, count it all joy when you fall into various trials, knowing that the testing of your faith produces patience. But let patience have its perfect work, that you may be perfect and complete, lacking nothing."* (James 1:2-4)

The trials associated with difficult circumstances produce

qualities that cannot be developed in any other way. As we walk through challenging circumstances with our eyes of faith focused on God, a good thing happens. Like the muscles of a weight lifter after a strenuous workout, our character is strengthened through adversity. Tough circumstances may leave us emotionally and spiritually exhausted, but the process works to produce greater strength of character.

James describes this process of shaping us into the likeness of God as a necessary work to make us complete. Each trial or circumstance works necessary qualities into our lives for completeness, so that nothing is lacking that is necessary to fulfill God's plan. A father who has embraced this process in his own life is equipped to recognize and support its work in his children's lives as well.

Character is developed and strengthened through an oftentimes painful process, one that all of us would like to avoid, whether children or adults. However, when the process has worked its way

Shielding your children from trials and difficult circumstances subverts the process of making them well-rounded individuals armed with the character of God.

to completion, it develops God's nature in us.

Character development is a step-by-step process. It takes time. Like a chef creating a culinary masterpiece, ingredients are added in measured amounts, not all at once, but at just the right time in the cooking process to produce a dish that delights the taste buds and satisfies the appetite. Character is created through a similar process. God measures out situations based on our level of maturity, adding complications at just the right moment to test our values, expose our weak areas, and ultimately round out our character. The process produces a masterpiece of individual character that is stronger and more complete than ever before.

We refer to a person who has been shaped by this process as a person who has "integrity," which means "incorruptibility and completeness." A person of integrity is a person who has well-rounded character.

Every day, situations arise that demand a response, and some are more difficult than others. The more difficult ones test the fiber of our being, exposing weaknesses and imperfections. This is how character is developed. Shielding our children from trials and difficult circumstances subverts the process of making them well-rounded individuals armed with the character of God. Parents who are not aware of this process are under the misconception that by defending their children, they are protecting them—when in actuality, they are subverting character development.

Parents play a beneficial roll when they work with their children to discover the lesson to be learned in a difficult situation rather than being their child's champion and defender against all perceived injustice. When there is physical danger or emotional abuse that goes beyond the discomfort of things not going their way, it is our responsibility as parents to step into the situation to protect our children. Otherwise, we need to work with our children to identify and embrace the situation as a developmental test from God. If we subvert the test, it just means they will have to take it over again using different circumstances.

Trinity Fellowship Church has a kindergarten through twelfth grade accredited school. During a period in the school history when the students were required to wear uniforms, the uniform policy stated that a uniform sweater was to be worn before a jacket for warmth and protection during cold or inclement weather.

One of the students wore a jacket to class during a period of cold winter weather. The classroom teacher reminded the student that the uniform policy required wearing a uniform sweater before wearing a jacket for warmth and asked her to remove her jacket while in class. The student objected, telling the teacher she didn't own a uniform sweater because her parents thought it was unnecessary. She refused to remove her jacket, stating she was too cold. The teacher, in response, sent her to the principle's office where the policy was enforced and she was made to remove the jacket before being allowed to return to class.

When she informed her parents of the situation that had developed during class, they were furious at the teacher and the school administration. They did not agree with the uniform policy and its enforcement by the teacher. The parents felt the teacher was heartless because she did not allow their daughter to be warm in class, even if it did violate the uniform policy.

The parents stepped in to right the injustice of the situation involving their daughter. They mounted a campaign to get the teacher removed and to get the policy overturned. They sought to organize a parent boycott of the school if the teacher and policy were not removed.

As you read this account you may side with the parents believing that the teacher was too rules-centered and insensitive to the physical need of a student in her class. You may also think that the parents did what was right in coming to the defense of their child. This type of response by parents is becoming more common in situations involving perceived injustice from authorities in their children's life. It is the response that subverts character development in our children.

From our adult experiences we know that life is not always fair. Most of us have experienced some form of injustice by authorities in our life. But in this case, there was *no* compelling reason for the parents to step in; no physical danger represented by the teacher's response, no emotional scar as a result of their daughter being cold in class. Discomfort yes, but compelling danger, no!

So what is the character issue involved in this situation? What should the parents have done to support the development of their child's character?

The issue being developed is submission to authority and faith in God, faith in His ability to bring justice to any situation. To support this important lesson first, they should have comforted their daughter, giving her the compassion she missed from the teacher and principle. Then they should have told their daughter that they would go out the next day and buy her a uniform sweater. They should have told her they made a mistake in not purchasing the uniform sweater when they purchased the other uniform pieces. In short, they should have supported the authority of the teacher and school administration to their daughter, thereby teaching her the importance of respect to authority. Finally, for their own strength of resolve in the situation they needed to maintain the perspective that God is able to change the situation they don't like while protecting their daughter—knowing He is able to right all injustice. The key is to respond with a right attitude.

LESSONS FORM CHARACTER

I learned an important lesson in character development at the age of thirteen, one which my dad could have easily subverted had he not reacted in the proper way.

It was summer, and I decided that I would mow lawns for extra money. With my parents' approval, I canvassed the neighborhood and soon found my first customer: a nice widow who lived behind the church parking lot next to our house. She was very particular in the way she kept her lawn. She expected the grass clippings to be carried to the trash, and the driveway and walks to be edged neatly. I quoted her my price, and the next day she called to find out how soon I could start.

"I have out-of-town guests coming to visit," she said, "and I want the lawn to look good for their arrival." We agreed on a date for me to begin servicing her lawn.

When the day arrived, I was out of the mood. A neighborhood baseball game at the elementary school by our house caught my interest, and I promptly forgot about my commitment to my customer, the condition of her lawn, and her out-of-town guests who were to arrive later that day.

That evening as we sat down to dinner, the widow's lawn was a distant memory in my mind. Then the telephone rang. It was my customer calling, demanding to know why I had not mowed her lawn. She was upset and disappointed.

Unfortunately, my dad had answered the call. When he discovered that I had failed to keep my word, he apologized to her, and told her that I would be right over to keep my end of the bargain.

I tried to convince my dad that I should cut my loss in this situation. "After all," I said, "I've messed up, and she's mad at me. Why should I go and confront her in her anger? Why not let her get someone else to mow her lawn? I can start fresh with a new customer another day."

My response so irritated my dad that he accompanied me over to the lady's house and stood there while I apologized. As I mowed, hauled the grass to the trash, and edged the walks, he and the lady critiqued my work while enjoying a neighborly conversation. When I finished, my dad made sure that I apologized again, and then he did something completely unexpected—*he refused to let her pay me*

> *...parents must be on watch and make the most of every opportunity to mold character.*

for the work!

To make matters worse, she told me that because I had not kept my word, she could not trust me, and therefore, would not keep me as her lawn boy. She concluded by telling me again how disappointed she was in me. This humiliating situation etched into my character a lesson of faithfulness that I have never forgotten.

I have observed many parents who react completely opposite of the way my dad reacted to my character failure. It is as if they condone and encourage character flaws. With co-dependent unhealthiness, they defend the incorrect behavior of their children, attacking the person who points out the flaw, and making them the issue, rather than requiring their children to correct their behavior. Sadly, when an opportunity is missed, not only is it gone, it's actually done harm to the child's character. Therefore, parents must be on watch and make the most of every opportunity to mold character.

A Lifelong Work

My dad's example benefited Jan and me many times over the years in rearing our family. Learning lessons of character helped me recognize opportunities to teach character to each of our children. Lessons of character continue to present themselves through a variety of situations that impact Jan and me individually, us as a couple, and each of our children. Character development is a lifelong work.

Each of our children has played some level of competitive sports. Athletics offer ample trials that test, mold, and perfect character. From playing time, to the coach's treatment, to personal discipline and diligent preparation, to maintaining the right attitude in competition, there are many opportunities to mold, shape, and strengthen character.

At a relatively young age our oldest son, Todd, had demonstrated above-average athletic ability. Beginning around age five I started working with him to develop his basketball skills. He was better than most of his peers and he loved the game. So when the morning of tryouts for the "Little Dribbler's" basketball team finally arrived, Todd was determined to make the team. Jan and I thought he was a cinch to be drafted because of his skill and the relationship we had with several of the coaches who would be drafting players for their team.

When the tryouts were completed and team selections were posted, Todd was not chosen. Disappointed and feeling the stun of rejection, he convinced himself that he had not been selected due to his lack of ability. His self-esteem plunged as he declared himself a terrible player. In addition, Jan and I were hurt and confused because he had not been selected, and we could not understand why. It was tempting to be angry and bitter, lashing out at people involved in the selection—but we knew this response was not right, nor would it help our son deal with his disappointment.

We were scrambling to make "lemonade" out of the "lemons" from this situation when a league official announced that a second league would be formed. The new league would incorporate all the boys who had not been selected to play in the original league; no one would be left out.

With some degree of coaxing on our part, our son agreed to play in what he called the "loser's" league. I told him he was a good player with good skills, and that he would most likely enjoy extra playing time in the new league, which he might not have enjoyed had he been selected to play on a team in the first draft. I encouraged him to work hard and do his best because I knew good things result when we make a proper response to circumstances. Both Jan and I assured him that diligent effort, a good attitude, patience, and steadfast commitment would pay off in the long run. How did we know? Because these are the qualities of character, and character always prevails!

Todd joined the new league and was an influential player. He was selected to the all-star team, and it ended as a good basketball experience. He went on to play high school basketball and was a varsity player during his junior and senior years. Upon graduation, he was selected to play on the regional all-star team. Diligence, good attitude, patience, and steadfast commitment had paid off well.

If I had not understood the potential impact of situations on the development of character, the basketball story would have been a painful family memory from our son's youth. However, because of our influence, the difficult situation ended with good results and produced some great basketball memories for our family. Memories are great, but more important are the qualities of character that are developed, tested, and tempered through trials. We must not rob our children of character development by shielding them from tough situations.

At all stages and ages of our children's development, situations will arise that seem unjust, unfair, cause hurt and tears, and overwhelm them, testing their ability to respond correctly. This situation was very traumatic for Todd, but not as traumatic as breaking up with his first girlfriend, or rear-ending another car at a stoplight totaling his car, or being detained at the airport security check point for his comment about a concealed weapon.

You may be facing circumstances or situations that are much

more severe than the issues I faced with Todd, but the truth of God's principles apply to every situation, and they will give you solid direction as you walk with your children through their difficulties, developing their character and deepening their trust in God.

TESTS OF CHARACTER NEVER STOP

I once heard someone say that God's tests are pass/fail, meaning you keep taking the test until you pass. Character development is not just for children; tests of character continue right through adulthood. In that sense, we have this in common with our children: God is still molding and developing our character, even as we are working with Him to shape theirs.

In the early years of my business career, I faced a test of character on the job. I was the assistant merchandising manager for one of my company's marketing regions. My department purchased all the products for the sales force to market in the company's southwest division. One of our largest customers was the state government and its related agencies. It was my responsibility to order products we sold to them under special pricing from our suppliers. It was also my responsibility to keep accurate records of purchases by the different agencies, quarterly reporting the sales volume associated with the state contract to our suppliers.

One morning, my boss walked into my office and asked me to place an order for 80,000 pounds of printing paper for one of our customers. As he left my desk to return to his office, he instructed me to enter the order as a state contract purchase. There was just one problem—that particular customer was not a state agency.

What was I to do? Ignore his request, or join in his dishonesty and enter the order? After an hour of internal struggle and debate— the nature of which tests the strength and integrity of personal character—I determined that I could not enter the order. If the order was to be entered, I resolved that my boss would have to enter it himself. I was prepared to stand my ground, even if it cost me my job.

Later in the day, my boss returned to my desk. I assumed he

wanted to check on the status of the order, but to my surprise and before I could tell him of my resolve, he said he had changed direction with the customer and would not need the order. As he rushed out of my office and on to his next appointment, he told me to cancel the order.

The test of my character in this situation was the process of thought that led me to the internal commitment to quit my job before lying to our supplier. With the commitment made, the action never materialized. In effect, it was a simulation. It looked real, felt real, and required a response as if it was real; but it never fully materialized.

Sometimes circumstances create a simulation to test character. In this case the conditions caused me to wrestle with issues in my heart that tested and revealed the qualities and strength of my character. Luckily, the process stopped short of requiring me to act on what I determined as the appropriate course of action during the test.

Airline pilots understand this type of training. They regularly have their flight skills tested and certified by being presented with very real flight situations through the use of a simulator. A simulator is a computerized apparatus that simulates conditions of flight and tests the pilot's ability to react to flight conditions. With an evaluator looking on, they respond to various situations that test their response to tough flight situations before they encounter them for real in the cockpit of a plane loaded with people.

We never know which test will include the requirement to act on what we have determined is right and which situation will end up being just a simulated test to check the reflexes of our character. Therefore, we must treat every test as though it is real and will require us to act on what we have determined is right.

Simulated or real, the issue is character—trained, prepared, and strengthened to meet the challenges of life. The work is done through the situations and circumstances that develop in everyday life! God is our evaluator in these tests, monitoring our thoughts and our intended actions. When we think and act correctly, it is like we have been certified as strong enough to withstand the amount of stress on our character that the situation has applied. The process has tested our character and it is certified by God to meet the challenge.

Concluding Thoughts

Character is developed by recognizing and using the daily tests of life to train, mold, and perfect specific qualities that are missing in our children's character. We must also understand that the tests change from year to year as our children mature.

It is important to teach our children to trust God above people, and develop in them the desire to choose right over wrong in the midst of circumstances, regardless of fairness or feelings. As we do this, we partner with God in His work to test, strengthen, and perfect our children's character. *"Train up a child in the way he should go,"* the Scripture says, *"And when he is old he will not depart from it."* (Proverbs 22:6)

CHAPTER 6

Faith's Influence on
Character Development

Regardless of the details, which are different in each circumstance, faith always asks for our response. Will it be a response of trust in God's faithfulness, or will it be a response that takes matters into our own hands? The answer to this question determines if faith comes alive in our circumstance to influence the outcome, or if it remains on the sidelines, never to be activated, never to make a difference.

Faith is confident trust in the character of God. In very practical terms, faith is like glasses used to correct vision. Through faith, we gain the ability to see God's work in all situations. Faith lays the foundation for trust in God. Faith is not driven or determined by emotions, but instead, faith is anchored to God's Word. Through faith, we gain God's perspective on situations, seeing them in a completely different light. Faith gives the ability to *know that we know that we know*—that God is working in our circumstances, even though our eyes may not see it and our logic may not be able to confirm the complete result. When faith is at work, it overrules feelings and frees us from anxiety, panic, or certain thoughts that battle for control of our lives, applying pressure on us to act independently of God and His will.

Notice that as I have defined faith, it has not been in the context of church attendance or a religious institution. You and I are people of faith not because we attend church or belong to a religious organization. We are people of faith because we see the connection

Through faith, circumstances don't rule us; we rule them.

of three interdependent truths: 1) God is present and intimately involved in the circumstances of life; 2) His promises are true and have universal application; and 3) Our sincere effort toward personal application of His promises will produce results in the circumstances of life. When actions are based on these precepts, faith acts as the rudder that steers the ship and the fuel that supplies its forward motion. It moves out of the realm of religious thought to be what God intended: an active agent that influences perspective and energizes behavior. Through faith, circumstances don't rule us; we rule them.

Parents enter into a partnership with God through faith using circumstances to fashion character in their children. Circumstances are the kiln used to bake the qualities of character to their finished strength and appearance. The "firing" process produces brilliantly glazed qualities of character such as honesty, truthfulness, diligence, loyalty, bravery, generosity, patience, the ability to receive correction, and more. When faith is added to any circumstance, it serves to provide protection for the vessel and ensure that damage does not occur in the "firing" process. Parents who attempt to create the qualities of character on their own, without the support of faith, must depend on their own wisdom and experience—something God never intended.

Walking by Faith!

Circumstances create opportunities for faith to influence our behavior. Faith also keeps us from responding to issues based on our feelings. Here is an example from our family:

The year that Jan and I celebrated our eighth anniversary; circumstances presented a critical need. Tyler, our third child, had made his entrance into our family, and our house had become cramped. We needed more living space to accommodate our growing family, so we began to seek God about moving. There was one major obstacle that stood in our road. The early 1980's were a time of double-digit inflation. Inflation was driving the purchase price of homes up steeply, and mortgage interest rates climbed right along with them. Although we felt God's release to begin looking for a new home for our family, the search was very frustrating. When we found a house that would meet our needs, the 18% mortgage interest rate made the payment out of the reach of our family budget. Jan's parents, knowing our need, made a generous offer of financial help to enable us to get into a larger home.

Finally our search turned up a "fixer upper" home comprised of everything we required: four bedrooms, an open and spacious kitchen, a large living area, and lots of storage. Although it needed to be updated, we were willing to fix it up because the condition brought the sales price into our price range. More importantly, the home had an assumable mortgage. In other words, it had a mortgage that could be assumed simply by paying the sellers their equity amount (the difference between the sales price and the mortgage amount of the note).

The money we needed to assume the seller's note exceeded the proceeds we were going to receive from the sale of our home, requiring a significant financial commitment from Jan's parents. Although we had not discussed the amount of their commitment, we moved forward. At the recommendation of our realtor, we decided to wait until our home sold before making a formal offer on the "fixer upper." Our realtor advised us that the sale of our home would allow us to offer a quick closing on the purchase, something she believed would be attractive to the seller, hopefully securing the lowest possible purchase price.

We set things in motion, believing God was answering our prayers. In a few days, our home sold for the full asking price. It so happened that the weekend our house sold, Jan's folks came for a visit. It seemed perfect to show them our "fixer upper" and talk about the specific details of the purchase contract.

Two obstacles developed that had to be overcome. First, as I previously mentioned, we had not discussed with Jan's parents the specific amount they would need to contribute to allow the purchase to take place. In the rush of activities surrounding the sale of our home and the purchase of our new one, Jan and I had assumed too much. When we finally sat down with Jan's parents to discuss the details, we found they had a different amount in mind than we did. Although we had been praying for God's leading in each decision regarding our move, the circumstances were changing, and things were not working out as we expected.

We were faced with a major question. Were we going to panic under what seemed to be the shakiness of the situation? Or, were we going to trust that God was working to bring about the right result? Regardless of the details, which are different in each circumstance, faith always asks for our response. Will it be a response of trust in God's faithfulness, or will it be a response that takes matters into our own hands? To answer faith's question with a decision to trust God, rather than take matters into our own hands tests qualities of character like honesty and faithfulness. The decision to trust God determines if faith comes alive in our circumstance to influence the outcome, or if it remains on the sidelines, never to be activated, never to make a difference.

When Jan and I realized the miscommunication between us and our parents and their discomfort with the financial amount we needed, we released them from any financial obligation associated with their offer. Our answer to faith's question in this circumstance was to trust God for His provision. He would be our resource, even though we did not know how. Our response released Jan's parents from the pressure they felt to meet our need due to the quick sale of our home. Like Abraham, the father of our faith, we headed out, not knowing where we were going, but trusting that God was directing the circumstances, and confident He would get us where we needed to go.

We had just answered faith's first question when the second obstacle presented itself. The "fixer upper" sold before we could make a formal offer on it! We had no place to go, with less money than expected, and a sales contract that gave the new owners possession of our house in 30 days. We needed answers! We needed to move!

"How could this be, God?" we thought. "How could we have missed Your direction this badly?"

We felt panic, but our faith overpowered our panic, orienting our perspective. We began to see that God had something different for us. Again, faith had presented its question, and our response was again to trust God and believe in His work before our eyes could see the reality of it. Our faith was grounded on the scripture that says: *"... your Father knows what you have need of before you ask Him."* (Matthew 6:8)

We were confident that God would lead us to a good place and teach us new things about Him in the process. Our attention turned toward building a new home. Jan looked through plans, and I began to search for a lot. We found a rental home for the interim. The rent was almost twice the amount of our old house payment— for much less house. Nevertheless, faith influenced our actions and gave us the perspective that God was leading us to a better place.

We were moving ahead with plans for a new home when a friend told us about a large, two-story house that had been on the market for some time. She encouraged us to take a look at it, and told us that we might be surprised to find it in our price range.

The house turned out to be bigger and better than the "fixer upper" we had not been able to purchase, and it was immediately available to move into. Through our realtor, we negotiated a purchase price with favorable financing terms, and moved into the house using only the equity from the sale of our home. God's hand was at work on our behalf.

God had guided our steps, and through actions of faith, we possessed the house that He had been preparing for us all along. As the icing on the cake, Jan's parents purchased new carpet for the entire house! The carpet was a very generous gift that enhanced the look of our new home and was more in line with their thinking when they made their offer to help. Everyone was pleased and we lived in that house for 20 years. It was God's blessing to us!

> *You must allow faith to determine your perspective in the circumstances of life, so you can influence and support God's work in the circumstances that your children will face.*

Once again, let me say that we can only transfer to our children what we possess for ourselves. We must allow faith to determine our perspective in the circumstances of life so that, through our experience, we can be in a position to influence and support God's work in the circumstances that our children will face in life. Faith anchors our character to God by keeping our attention and dependence focused upon Him.

Faith's Influence

Is God at work in every situation? This must be our understanding and our perspective for faith to have its proper influence. Jesus told His disciples not to worry about the circumstances and needs of their lives. He assured them that God knew their situation, along with their needs, so they could have confidence that He would care for them (Luke 12:22-34).

I know this truth, I believe it, and attempt to apply it to my perspective in every circumstance. However, there are times when I need my wife or a close friend to remind me of this truth, encourage me in the situation, and bolster my faith by inserting some of their faith where mine has become weak. This is especially true when I have not seen any change to my situation although I have been waiting for a long time.

At these times I need the strength and influence of someone else's faith to encourage, strengthen, and bolster mine. Because I am aware of this need in my life, I am sensitive to the fact that my children also have this need in their life. It is my God-ordained responsibility as their father to influence their perspective with my faith.

Several years ago, as I enjoyed my morning quiet time on a trip, my thoughts were centered on my oldest daughter, Lisa, who was attending the University of Nebraska in Omaha. She was dating a young man who had graduated from college and was pursuing his career. I had concerns about the relationship. I worried that they might get serious about marriage without addressing important issues in their relationship. I was concerned that Lisa might compromise the qualities she really wanted in her husband just to be married.

I was praying about my concerns as I read my Bible and wrote in my journal. Lisa was on my heart. I felt like the Lord gave me a message for her, so I recorded the impression in my journal. Later that day, I called Lisa to talk, as I did regularly, and her dating situation came up in our conversation. I took the opportunity to tell her about the message the Lord gave that morning. It went something like this: He wanted her to know that if she would not compromise her standard for a husband, He would bring her husband to her at the right time. I told her this word was a promise for her, to be remembered as she dated and considered marriage. The promise was this: God would bring her the husband of her dreams, a man prepared by God to meet her needs, if she would patiently wait for Him to finish His work. This special man would not require her to compromise her standards, or lessen her desires related to a husband. God was preparing him to meet her needs and fulfill all her dreams. Jeremiah 29:11 says:

> *"For I know the thoughts that I think toward you, says the LORD, thoughts of peace and not of evil, to give you a future and a hope."*

Confident that the message represented God, I delivered it to her with passion and conviction. I was well aware that something like this could be contrived in my mind as a way to manipulate her to a desired action. I was careful to check my own motives and make sure that God had initiated the message, not a manipulative father. As I prayerfully reevaluated the message and my motive, I knew the message was true and that it represented God's heart. I knew God to provide hope and to encourage confidence in His care, because I had experienced it in my own life. The message renewed Lisa's willingness to be patient; it brought encouragement to her heart, giving her a perspective of faith, and enabling her to trust God while waiting patiently for His work on her behalf to be completed. Three years later, God was true to His word: *He brought her the man whom He had prepared especially for her. We are proud to have him in our family. As they were married in December of 1999.*

Nurturing Faith in Your Circumstance

Faith that is alive and active, faith that influences your perspective and energizes your behavior, does not come from religious activity or discipline. It is nurtured *through relationship.*

The Apostle Paul had this kind of one-on-one relationship with God, writing in Galatians 2:20:

> *"...Christ lives in me; and the life which I now live in the flesh, I live by faith in the Son of God, who loved me and gave Himself for me."*

Everyone can have this kind of faith! It is not reserved for an elite few! God has made it available to all who desire to involve Him in the daily aspects of their living!

Welcome Christ into your circumstances today, and allow Him to walk with you. Give Him the authority to determine your future. He will relate to you in a personal way through the presence of the Holy Spirit, and your faith will be activated as we have discussed in this chapter. Don't wait; welcome Him into your circumstances today!

Concluding Thoughts

Faith is more than a mental assent to a set of values. It is a system of beliefs that become the motivation for action. Faith is an essential tool in our parenting partnership with God. In fact, the only way to partner with God is through faith (Hebrews 11:6).

Are you attempting to raise your children without a partnership between you and God? Do you possess a dynamic interactive faith that determines perspective and influences your behavior?

Make your relationship with God intimate and personal by regularly seeking Him with all your heart. Wait expectantly on Him, and with resolute determination, search for Him in every situation involving you and your children. **Actively apply all the promises of God's Word to your circumstances, allowing faith to orient and influence your perspective, and you will witness miraculous results.**

CHAPTER 7

The Components of Balanced Discipline
Part 1 – Submission to Authority

*True submission does not require
mindless, blind loyalty to the commands
and whims of the person in charge. True
submission is revealed in the response to a
person of authority and leadership.*

Lawlessness, independence, and rebellion have become the behavioral norm in our society. A self-centered culture all about "me" is swallowing up the love and self-sacrifice that God intended for humanity to express toward each other. Our society's creed has become, *"I want what I want, when I want it...and nothing should stop me from getting it!"*

The spirit of lawlessness embodied by this selfish attitude has existed upon the earth since the fall of satan. However, it has intensified over the millennia of man's presence on earth and is today inflicting destructive havoc everywhere we look in society. It is a spiritual attack on God's most precious creation—humanity.

America has now produced three generations that have grown up without a model of submission and personal sacrifice. Since World War II, children have witnessed a diminishing response of corrective discipline and accountability. Schools have become hotbeds of violence. Juvenile detention centers are over-flowing. Lawlessness, rebellion, and independence rule as never before.

Parents, government leaders, educational institutions, media conglomerates, social service organizations, and law enforcement agencies grope for solutions to these very serious and growing problems. Of course, the answer is right under their nose, yet our leaders are either unwilling or unable to accept the solution or recognize what is needed to solve the lawlessness. Though readily available, the anti-virus for society's plague is ignored.

The Answer to Lawlessness

How can we begin to stem the tide of lawlessness in our society? How can we establish order in our homes and schools? The solution being ignored is simple*: we must submit to authority, embrace discipline, and allow someone who loves us to scrutinize our actions and keep us accountable.*

This simple solution cuts across the grain of thinking in America. The mantra today is that submission, discipline, and accountability are old-fashioned, intolerant, and out of step with modern society. "Personal responsibility" has been removed from the vocabulary of our culture. Laws are in place to make spanking a criminal offense. We are substituting corrective discipline with "time-outs" in our families and in our society believing that if we

...we must submit to authority, embrace discipline, and allow someone who loves us to scrutinize our actions and keep us accountable.

distract the action we will change the behavior. Using that theory we have targeted guns for removal so violence will diminish. We have placed x-ray machines at the entrances of schools, amusement parks, and sporting events to protect participants rather than penalizing the lawless when caught. These efforts are restricting personal freedoms of the individual rather than holding each person responsible for their behavior.

Once again the principle of transference comes into play. We cannot expect our children to take responsibility for their behavior and actions, if we as their parents will not take responsibility for our actions and behavior. We can't transfer to our children what we will not embrace ourselves. If we will take an honest look, we see how deeply rooted this problem of independence and blame shifting is in the fabric of our lives! It covers a broad spectrum of behavior from simple relatively harmless mistakes to tragic errors in judgment.

When our youngest daughter Lindsay started driving, Jan and I decided that we would take advantage of the option to do parent supervised driver education. This was a new program, offered to parents through the State Department of Public Service, and was recognized by the auto insurance carriers within our state. One morning as I was giving Lindsay "in car" driving instruction, she approached an intersection coming to a stop at the corner.

She made a rolling stop quickly turning onto the street in front of an on coming car. The car that she cut off switched lanes and honked at her as it passed her in the other lane. She was furious at the other driver for honking at her. I explained to her that she had cut him off in her rush to turn from the side street into traffic. She objected, not at all acknowledging her error, but remaining upset at the other driver the rest of the way to school. In her mind she did nothing wrong – after all - there was no accident; the other driver just had a problem. This is a simple example of the way we refuse to take responsibility for our behavior and shift the blame to someone else.

In Florida there was the case of Lionel Tate, the 12-year-old boy that killed a friend in 1999 while practicing wrestling moves he saw on television. This case reveals the other end of the spectrum. It was a tragic error in judgment by Lionel Tate thinking he could demonstrate the wrestling moves he saw on a younger and smaller friend. It was even more tragic for six-year-old Tiffany Eunick (and her parents) who died as a result of Lionel's action.

The jury in the case convicted Lionel of 2nd degree murder, and he was sentenced to life in prison. Following his conviction and during his trial, blame was pointed at pro wrestling for giving him the idea for the moves he was practicing, to the prosecutor who filed the charges, to the judge who tried the case. The common assessment by the media and others familiar with the situation was this death could not have been all Lionel Tate's fault—someone else had to be at fault because Lionel was too young.

From the simple to the tragic, the response is the same—we are unwilling to accept responsibility for the results of our behavior so we attempt to shift the blame to another person.

The Subtleties of the Problem

The spirit of lawlessness has these two responses as its tap root: the unwillingness to take responsibility for behavior and the shifting of blame. Through the subtle working of these two responses the spirit of lawlessness hypnotizes our thinking and secures its deadly hold. In subtle ways it permeates our thinking and perspective across a broad spectrum of behaviors. Its hypnotic hold is introduced so surreptitiously that it can go almost undetected.

My dad had always known the importance of discipline in child development. He consistently administered loving correction to my sisters and me as we grew up, held us accountable for our actions, and taught us to submit to authority.

When I was in junior high, in the mid-60s, the Beatles introduced their look to America's youth. I liked them, and grew my hair "Beatles-style"—combed over my ears with long bangs.

Although I made good grades and was not a troublemaker at school, I was called to the principal's office because my hair violated school policy. The principal sent me home, telling me that I could not come back until I had my hair cut. I protested, based on my good behavioral and academic record. I believed being a good student behaviorally and academically should make my hair length a non-issue. He didn't buy it, and sent me home.

My mom was surprised to see me come home early. After I explained the situation, she dropped me off at the barbershop to get the haircut necessary to comply with the principal's demand. I told the barber that I just wanted a light trim. "Don't take off too much," I said, and he willingly complied.

The next day, I presented my new haircut to the principal for inspection. To my complete frustration, my new haircut didn't pass! He sent me home again!

"I am never going back to that school!" I announced to my mom as I walked in the door. "They have no right to make me shave my head!" My interpretation was a slight exaggeration of school policy.

My mom allowed me to fume until my dad came home. When he arrived, I told him my side of the story and he listened patiently, nodding his head and acknowledging with a periodic "ah-huh," which led me to believe that he was agreeing with me.

When I finished, he stood and motioned me to the garage. In the garage, he motioned for me to get in the car. Then he drove me to the barbershop, walked me in, and *he* told the barber how to cut my hair. My dad explained to me that I would submit to the authority of the school and my principal. He told me that the principal's request was within his realm of authority, and it did not matter if we agreed. With a good attitude, we would do as the principal had asked. Through loving correction and accountability during my childhood, my dad taught me to submit to authority. His instruction included the truth that submission is not based upon agreement.

Years later, as an adult, I saw how the lawless spirit of this age had seduced even the resolute determination of my own father. One afternoon, Jan and I along with Todd, who was a toddler at the time, were visiting my mom and dad. We were inexperienced parents, but had committed to train our children through loving discipline as our parents had trained us. This discipline included spankings, which served to get our child's attention as it taught him to obey.

As my dad and I talked in their family room that summer day, Todd became fascinated with a floor fan circulating the air in the room. Slowly, curiously, he worked his way toward the fan for a closer look. As he did, I said to him, "No, no."

The first time or two that I called him, I would stand and bring him back to me, turning his attention away from the fan. Each time, however, he would return his attention to the fan. The third time I called him, he hesitated as before, but then turned and proceeded toward the fan. He was old enough to understand me, and had minded my "no, no's" in other situations, however, not this time. I stood from my chair and swatted him two times on the bottom. The process was quick; it pained his little ego more than his bottom, and stopped him dead in his tracks. I left him in a pile of tears on the floor between the fan and my chair. I sat down again, and called to him to come to me so that I could comfort and love him. He sat there, his pitiful eyes looking for sympathy. In the most dramatic fashion, his eyes appealed to his grandpa, who had observed the event from the chair next to mine. Compassion arose in my dad that I could not remember from my childhood years. He looked at me and said, "We should have moved the fan. He was just curious."

I had to defend myself, and remind my dad that parents should not cater to disobedience, even if it is driven by curiosity. "The fan does not need to be moved," I said. "My son needs to be trained to obey."

My dad reluctantly agreed, somehow forgetting his years of

similar training that he had extended to my sisters and me.

Children learn to manipulate others and generate sympathy early in life. When Todd's appeal did not work, he responded to my encouragement, coming to me for love and assurance. He never went back to the fan.

As we said good-bye to my parents at the door, my dad gave me a big hug and whispered in my ear, "And don't spank my grandbaby any more!" Oh, how the roles change from parent to grandparent!

I bent down and hoisted my dad over my shoulder like he was a big sack of potatoes, carried him to the front yard and twirled him around, returning him somewhat dizzy to the ground. This little demonstration between father and son reminded him that I was old enough—and strong enough—to be the dad, and that I would teach my children to obey without losing my temper, as he had taught me.

My dad knew the importance of discipline in molding the character of children. Yet the subtle tentacles from the spirit of lawlessness had worked their way into my dad's thinking as his response changed from parent to grandparent. Almost imperceptibly, these tentacles were attempting to change the process of discipline so necessary for equipping our next generation with the tools for success. Our playful interchange in the front yard was my effort to expose and unwrap the deceptive tentacles of the spirit of lawlessness from our relationship. I wanted and expected my parents to support the work of discipline in their grandchildren.

...you have as much authority to transfer the benefits of discipline to your children as you have properly responded to the discipline of the authorities in your life.

A Three-Pronged Attack on Lawlessness

When we talk about discipline, we are really referring to three connected and interdependent concepts: 1) *submission;* 2) *correction that includes punishment; and* 3) *accountability.* Without a proper understanding of each, the Bible's presentation of discipline cannot be fully understood. Each is a connected piece of the whole subject of discipline.

In this chapter, we will look at the first concept, submission. In the next two chapters, we will "complete the discussion" with an explanation of the other two concepts associated with discipline. Remember, the cardinal rule in parenting is the principle of transference, which says that you can only transfer what you have— and practice—in your own life. As we begin our look at discipline, I must ask you to scrutinize yourself as you read so that you can discipline your children in the proper spirit. Another way to look at the effect of transference is to say: you have as much authority to transfer the benefits of discipline to your children as you have properly responded to the discipline of the authorities in your life. With that in mind, let me ask you, how do you respond to correction? Your attitude toward submission and your response to correction will form the foundation for the training of your children.

What is Submission?

Submission is the decision to place yourself under the authority of another person or entity for correction and direction. Many equate submission with agreement. By contrast, true submission is actually revealed in disagreement. True submission does not require mindless, blind obedience to the commands and whims of the person in charge. True submission is revealed in one's response to a person of authority and leadership.

It is impossible to fully understand and walk in submission without the knowledge of, and confidence in, God's sovereignty. Men will fail in leadership positions, they will operate with impure motives that hurt and abuse others, and they will make unintentional mistakes that bring painful consequences. Our submission then, is not first and foremost to men. It is to God, who works through imperfect men to reveal and produce His will, and to protect those submitted to Him.

I submit to those in authority over me because the Bible tells me God places them in their authority. Romans 13:1-2 says:

> *"Let every soul be subject to the governing authorities. For there is no authority except from God, and the authorities that exist are appointed by God. Therefore whoever resists the authority resists the ordinance of God, and those who resist will bring judgment on themselves."*

Our superiors are worthy of respect due to God's appointment and placement of them, not because they have earned a seal of approval. Of course, we should only submit to direction that is legal, moral, and that agrees with God's law. In my life, most of the difficult situations that arise requiring my submission meet those criteria. The only situation in my adult experience that would have justified my resistance to submission is the situation I told in the last chapter. It involved a situation where my boss asked me to lie in placing an order for a customer. Since it involved a state contract I felt his request compromised my integrity and put me in potential legal jeopardy. I determined I would not comply with his request, even if it cost me my job.

Almost every situation requiring submission becomes a battle of the mind. When faced with such situations, I find myself attempting to categorize every situation as illegal, immoral, or in disagreement with God's law so that I can do what I want rather than properly submit.

I know what I am saying is hard, and I've struggled to get this right at times. But when I blow it, I always find myself in the middle of correction by God's hand. One such instance occurred as I fulfilled my duties as a pastor. Our church has been in a constant state of growth. From our beginning in 1978 we have grown to more than 7,000 members, and the ministries of the church have far-reaching influence. During one growth spurt, we needed expanded facilities for our youth. We found a vacant Quonset-style steel building once used for a roller-skating rink. We leased it and began remodeling the interior to serve the needs of our youth. I supervised the project, providing direct oversight to the project manager, who was a paid staff member of the church.

As with many construction projects, this one involved some unforeseen work, and in the finishing stages, it was over budget and past the completion deadline. For several weeks in a row our senior pastor, who was my boss, had directed me to bring the project to completion. He instructed me to finish the work in process and to delay anything not already begun. However, new "mini-projects" kept developing that took their place in the line of items required to bring the project to completion. Each week, I explained to him why the project had not been completed, providing him with details of the mini-projects. Each week, he instructed me to finish and to not start any new projects. After several weeks of this scenario, my work was brought into question. I justified the extension of the project with this attitude: if he were responsible for the work, he would understand that the mini-projects were necessary to bring the full project to completion.

The project was brought to a completion. However, at my year-end review I was corrected, and my salary increase for the next year was adjusted. I felt the correction was unfair; I felt I had been misunderstood. As others in leadership became aware of my correction, I was embarrassed. I felt *if I could explain myself in full detail,* telling about the "mini" projects, *all would be able to see that I was not the problem; it was the nature of the project!*

My pride was hurt, and in my mind I began the justification for my action, even giving thought to resigning. I thought about gathering a few of those close to me, in positions of influence to plead my case. As I contemplated those options, the Lord broke into my consciousness and spoke to my heart a very clear question, He said to me, "Are you going to let Me correct you?"

"Yes, Lord," I said immediately. "But You know all the details about the mini-projects. Surely You understand, correction is not needed."

He continued, "Then receive this correction and submit to the authority I have placed over you, and do it with a good attitude! You did not do as you were directed; you were rebellious in your heart to the direction of your boss, no excuses."

"Yes, Lord, I receive your correction. I am sorry," was my response.

I chose this example to present two important concepts related to submission. The first one is that everyone, regardless of age or responsibilities, is under someone's authority—*everyone!* Authority in our lives is as sure as death and taxes. The question we must

> *Your response to earthly authority— whether it is a response of submission or a response of rebellious independence— is your response to God's authority.*

answer is: How will we relate and respond to authority? Will we submit, or will our actions be independent and rebellious?

Secondly, if we do not submit to God's appointed earthly authority, then we will not submit to God either. Remember what Romans 13:2 says:

> *"Therefore whoever resists the authority resists the ordinance of God, and those who resist will bring judgment on themselves."*

Some who claim to love God and serve Him are rebellious. They act independent of His appointed authority in their lives. Our response to earthly authority, whether it is a response of submission or a response of rebellious independence, is our response to God's authority. It does not matter how our mind might justify the action; rebellious independence is wrong. However, a submitted response pleases God and brings His favor (1 Peter 2:18).

Concluding Thought

Submission is a critical concept for living. It forms the foundation for God's work and blessing in our lives. In our discussion, has the Lord revealed some action or attitude related to submission in your life? Perhaps you have recognized that your father's discipline was negligent, that it fostered lawlessness in your attitude toward submission. Or perhaps you have gained new understanding related to the concepts of submission and the connective foundation it provides for the whole structure of discipline.

As God has brought enlightenment to you through this chapter, it is important to make the appropriate response to Him. Repent for any acts of rebellion or independence. If specific instances come to mind, simply acknowledge your behavior or attitude as wrong.

Commit today to live in submission to all authority in your life—that of your government, employer, pastor, and parents. Become accountable to an individual or a group of men who love God, and who will love you.

You may feel discomfort at first as you make changes in your life, but don't allow negative feelings or thoughts to stop you from taking action. Your response will bring you blessing and change your whole approach to corrective discipline, forming the foundation for understanding and the authority to bring proper correction to your children.

CHAPTER 8

Components of Balanced Discipline
Part 2—Corrective Discipline

God's motive for correction is love;
His reason is always redemptive.
He disciplines us to rescue us from a
terrible fate, as He knows that
sin snowballs over time into an
avalanche of misery.

Discipline involves three connected and interdependent concepts: 1) *submission;* 2) *correction that includes punishment;* and 3) *accountability.* Without a proper understanding of each, the Bible's presentation of discipline cannot be fully understood. Each is a connected piece of the whole. To emphasize one over the others or to exclude one in favor of another will produce imbalanced and ineffective training to our children.

In the previous chapter, we discussed the importance of submission. In the next two chapters, we will "complete the circle" with a presentation and an explanation of the remaining two concepts: corrective discipline and accountability.

Keep two things in mind as you read this chapter. First, God has made men the manager of their home (see 1 Corinthians 11:3) and because of this He will hold them responsible for establishing a standard of values for their family and for implementing them in a manner consistent with His nature. The principle is revealed in the parable Jesus told his disciples in Luke, Chapter 16. In the parable a certain rich man (representing God) entrusted his possessions to a manager (representing us). It was reported to the rich man that his manager was mismanaging his possessions. The passage says the rich man called his manager and said to him, 'What is this I hear about you? Give an account of your management..."

Men as leaders and managers of their home will be called on to give an account of how they managed their family. Therefore, we must set the parameters for behavior, model then in our own behavior, and work to graciously transfer them in our children. Our reaction or indifference to issues that confront the family and its individual members will have a dramatic influence on the future atmosphere in our home along with influencing the behavior of each member of our family.

Many men leave the responsibility for correction to their wives. In doing so, these fathers shirk from their God-given responsibility to lead their families, missing the opportunity to be the influence God intended as He established His pattern for the family.

Secondly, remember the principle of transference, which says that you can only transfer what you have—and practice—in your own life. Once again as you read this chapter, take some time to scrutinize your actions before you attempt to influence your children's behavior through discipline. Remember, you must model the standard before you can transfer it to your children.

The Purpose of Correction

God's motive for correction is love; His reason is always redemptive. He disciplines us to rescue us from a terrible fate, as He knows that sin snowballs over time into an avalanche of misery. Therefore, His correction is always a blessing. Though painful for the moment, it is administered with a long-term perspective in mind.

Many parents lose or never even have this perspective in disciplining their children. Their discipline becomes motivated by something other than the future result of their children's behavior. Instead, their motivation for discipline becomes anger, frustration, embarrassment, impatience, or inconvenience; it is rarely motivated by thoughts of the long-term results of the behavior being corrected.

God's help combined with our diligent effort will establish a gracious standard, correct wrong behavior, and transfer His nature—instead of our imperfections—to our children.

The emotions created by their children's behavior lead to an effort to establish authority, demonstrate power, or maintain control. When parents allow pride, ego, authority, or position to motivate correction, they miss the real purpose of discipline. As a result, the discipline becomes abusive and harsh.

The most important function of a father is to demonstrate the nature and character of God to his wife and children. As fathers, we of course cannot measure up to God's perfect nature, but as we make an honest effort to do so, His grace covers our shortcomings. His help combined with our diligent effort will establish a gracious standard, correct wrong behavior, and transfer His nature, instead of our imperfections, to our children.

What Method of Correction Is Appropriate?

A variety of discipline methods are effective. The situation should determine the specific method used to bring correction. Consider God's discipline. He is patient and always kind. He is punitive with rebellion and disobedience, but quick to forgive, never withdrawing relationship when we acknowledge the wrong, ask forgiveness, and change our attitude or behavior. The method we use to bring correction should represent His manner of bringing correction to us.

Is Spanking Appropriate?

I realize that spanking is quite controversial as a method of correction. Today, our society frowns upon spanking for two reasons. First, it is often used to punish rather than correct. There is a significant difference between the two. Second, the prevailing thought in society is that humanity's intelligence has progressed to the point that it has surpassed the wisdom of the Bible, which makes strong statements regarding the connection between spanking and correction, like the one in Proverbs 13:24:

> *"He who spares his rod hates his son, but he who loves him disciplines him promptly."*

Spanking is thought of by some as harsh, punitive, and almost barbaric. I strongly disagree with this perspective. Spanking should never be done in an abusive manner. If it is administered wrongly, it can be damaging. So, let me present my perspective on spanking as a method of correcting and explain the way I corrected my children. I will show how it can be done so as to produce correction, and I will give the specific steps that must be taken to guard against abuse.

Jan and I used spanking to train our children. Spanking creates an association between pain and disobedience in our children's minds. My firm belief is that a spanking applied to the padded part of a child's bottom produces pain without physical or emotional damage. The pain helps teach the children two important concepts necessary for training to be effective:

1. It teaches a child to recognize that obedience is a choice.
2. It teaches a child to associate disobedience with painful consequences.

When done correctly, spanking develops a sense of responsibility in them for their actions. Their little instinct takes over, and self-preservation encourages obedience.

Pain by itself, however, does not produce correction, especially when the motive is self-serving to the parent. Spanking out of anger or frustration, or on places other than the padded part of a child's bottom, does not produce the corrective result we are seeking, and it risks injury to the child. The result is physical abuse which is the direct opposite of God's intended purpose. Any parent who physically damages a child and thinks the punishment will change behavior does not understand God's view of correction.

When our children were old enough to understand "no," we began spanking them when they disobeyed. At first, we used a pat on the hand to correct them for touching or grabbing something against our instruction. When that was no longer effective, Jan or I used a swat with our hand on their diaper-padded rear. As they grew a day came when the swat by hand failed to accomplish the correction we sought; the next step was to spank them with a wooden spoon or paddle. Never did we swat or spank on the legs or upper body, only on the bottom.

Your child's reaction will help identify the type of spanking method to use and when to change to a new method. A steely-eyed defiance that tells you "that didn't hurt" is the indication it is time to make a change in your method.

When we spanked our children, we always followed the same routine. Inconsistency is the enemy of discipline, so we always followed the same four steps as we administered a spanking, without compromise or wavering. Here are the four steps we followed so you can also follow them with your children:

1. *__Do not spank in anger.__* If we were angry or frustrated, we sent our child to the bedroom to wait for us. This gives them time to consider their behavior, and gives us time to take a deep breath and regain our composure before correcting them.

2. *__Spank in private.__* Correction is a private matter and should never be used to embarrass a child. As such, we never spank our children in front of friends, siblings, other adults, or in a public place.

3. *__Explain the offense before spanking.__* In the privacy of a bedroom or secluded place, we always asked our children to tell us the reason they are getting a spanking. Almost without fail, the response was, "I don't know." We have learned that a child must understand the reason for discipline in order for the correction to have proper influence on behavior. A brief explanation from them will reveal their level of understanding. If a child cannot explain what he did wrong, we must explain the unacceptable behavior in a way he can understand.

4. *__Administer pain not abuse.__* The purpose of spanking is to help our children associate disobedience with pain not to create fear in them. If these steps are followed your children will not cower in your presence, nor fear your wrath but they will learn to respond obediently to your direction. As previously stated, I do not believe you should spank in anger nor should the punishment be administered to other parts of the body except the padded part of the child's bottom.

The Response We Want From Our Children

In addition to these steps for us to follow when disciplining our children, Jan and I also required three responses from our children when they were disciplined. Here are the responses we required from our children and recommend they be required of your children when they receive your disciple:

1. _Be able to explain the offense_. As stated in step #3 above, we want our children to explain in their own words how they disobeyed. Disobedience is always the reason for correction. We need to know that they know what part of their behavior disobeyed our direction. They were not allowed to be mad at us or go silent in response to our correction.

2. _Show genuine sorrow for disobedience_. One important way that they indicate sorrow is in the attitude with which they receive correction. We wanted our children to understand that our motive for correction is the same as God's motive: _our love for them_. Before correction, we reminded our children that we do not let them disobey because of our love for them. We tell them that by learning to obey us, they learn to obey God. It is important, we told them, to learn to obey so that when they leave home and have a family of their own, they will obey God and live under His authority.

3. _Demonstrate affection toward the parent who spanked them_. After the spanking, we allowed a short time of demonstrative response to ease the pain. This includes dancing, bun-holding, or dropping to the floor into a pile of emotions. However, we didn't allow their response to be prolonged, overly dramatic, or an angry display of aggression toward us for the correction. Finally, the correction is not complete until our child accepts physical and emotional comfort from the disciplining parent. The comfort usually consists of a hug or a hug and a kiss between both parties.

On occasion, one of our children would refuse to come for love and comfort to the disciplining parent. Instead, they looked to the non-disciplining parent to give them comfort. When pride has suffered a blow, it is natural to be defiant or to reject the person bringing the correction, and to sport a bad attitude about the whole process of correction. Nevertheless, our response was the same: We would wait and insist on the giving and acceptance of love. We would not leave the place of correction until love was demonstrated.

> ### *God doesn't use our failures to condemn and reject us, so we do not want to do that to our children.*

If one step is missed more than any other when parents discipline their children; it is the step of affection. When anger or frustration has been the catalyst for the correction, rejection is the easiest response to reinforce our displeasure. So we spank them, send them to their room, or allow them to walk away in shame. We must avoid this response.

Jan and I never ignored or eliminated the step of affection, nor did we tell our children to "go to your bedroom to think about what you have done," which only serves to shame them for unacceptable behavior. Shame does not produce correct behavior. A spanking—not shame, not rejection—is the penalty for disobedience.

When the three-step process is complete, all is forgiven and we walk forward without pointing to the correction as a reminder of their failure or constantly referring back to the correction. The Bible tells us when we have received God's correction, He removes our sin as far as the east is from the west (Psalm 103:12). God doesn't use our failures to condemn and reject us, so we do not want to do that to our children.

What About Time-outs, Grounding, and Other Diversions?

Many parents use "time-out" as a replacement for spanking in their children's pre-teen years. While spanking is not the only method of correction parents have at their disposal, it should not be replaced or eliminated in favor of other methods like the "time-out," for the reason stated in Proverbs 13:24, mentioned earlier in this chapter. Spanking in their pre-teen years teaches children that they are responsible for their actions and greatly reduces discipline problems in their teen years.

I believe the use of a time-out can be effective when young children become so frenzied that they are not paying attention to instructions. Used in this manner, it gives children an opportunity to think more clearly, stop their activity so they can listen and respond from a more rational state. It allows them an opportunity to choose to obey. When used in this manner, a time-out can be effective as an intervening step before a spanking is administered. It gives children a chance to slow down, pay attention, and change their behavior. However, if they fail to take advantage of this cautionary step, they need to be spanked. A further time-out will not produce the correction that is needed.

Correcting Teenagers

In their early teens, our children had reached a physical size that made spanking almost impossible and in reality no longer effective. We still administered correction, but at that age we found that removing privileges more effectively reinforced our correction. As children move into their teen years, something happens. I call it the "Timex Factor." Like the famous watch, teens can "take a lickin' and keep on tickin'!"

"Grounding," or withholding privileges, administers a pain more effective than spanking. It involves denying the teen a privilege, such as being with friends, talking on the phone, using the Internet, driving, or attending special events.

We have been careful in the way we have administered grounding, because it must be tailored to the specific personality and interests of each child. What is effective for one child is wasted upon another. The duration and frequency must be considered carefully. Used improperly, grounding can quickly lose its corrective benefit and become a greater punishment to parents than it is to their children! When this happens, parents become inconsistent in enforcing the grounding, and the corrective benefit is lost. Teens

Correcting an attitude will expose a problem before it becomes a behavioral pattern.

quickly learn that the grounding won't stick, and they develop an attitude of indifference, even defiance toward the grounding.

Attitudes Are the Seeds of Behavior

Jesus taught principles using parables or short stories. One of His common themes emphasized that a person's actions originate from thoughts (Matthew 15:19). This is a powerful truth. The process of thoughts that leads to behavior is what psychologists call "acting out." Jesus taught that ultimately, we are what we think and encouraged us to be careful to guard our thoughts.

Attitudes reside in our hearts and influence our thinking. Our thinking determines our behavior. Therefore, we must correct both behavior and attitudes. *Correcting an attitude will expose a problem before it becomes a behavioral pattern.*

Our third child, Tyler, was a fun, funny, happy-go-lucky child, with an intense loyalty and a strong sense of fairness. Tyler was so adaptable that most of the time we wouldn't know the strength of his feelings or opinions. When he was in the third grade, we transferred him along with his older sister, Lisa, to a private Christian school.

During the first two weeks at the new school, Tyler complained that the school rules were unfair. For example, the school rules instructed children to keep their hands to themselves. Children were not allowed to run their hands along the hall walls, bother other people, or touch things that were not theirs. Dress codes and other rules were strictly enforced.

One day, Tyler came home and announced that he had encountered the most ridiculous and unreasonable rule yet. In fact, this rule was so unfair that he wanted out of "that crummy school." I could hardly wait to hear what was so unreasonable.

"One of my friends got swats for yawning in class!" he told me. "*Yawning in class*, Dad! Can you *believe that?*" ("Swats" is a term for spanking.)

I quizzed him a little further, quite certain that he might have overlooked an important detail or two.

"Well," he responded, "the teacher did tell him to cover his mouth when he yawned. But come on, Dad...is that ridiculous or *what?*"

As he responded, it dawned on me that he had an attitude of independence. He didn't like someone telling him or his friend what to do. In the public school system, Tyler's attitude of independence went unchallenged. Standards of behavior were different, and teachers had more kids to monitor than the teachers in the private school. Under tighter controls and a smaller student-teacher ratio, Tyler's independent attitude popped out.

Over the years of my pastoral ministry I have had the opportunity to know many families and watch them mature. I have been able to watch children develop from birth through adulthood. One young man came into the world with an attitude. He was cranky and fussy as a baby, and even in happy times, he was demanding.

When he was a toddler he was rough with his toys and with his friends never treating them with respect or care. His rough attitude and behavior carried across all ages of his development. When something broke due to his lack of care or abuse he expected his parents to get it fixed or replace it immediately. He was hard to live with until his desire was fulfilled. You might say he was spoiled!

I was puzzled as I watched how his parents reacted to his behavior. From preschool age right through his early twenties, they coddled his behavior and selfish attitudes. Making excuses like; "We kept him up past his nap time;" "He hasn't been feeling well;" "This has been a rough week for him," but rarely addressing or correcting his attitude or behavior.

When this boy was in his upper teens, he and some friends took the family boat to the lake for a day of fun. The boys started doing some dangerous stunts involving the use of the boat. During one of the stunts, they hit something submerged in the water knocking a hole in the boat. It took on water and quickly sank. None of the boys were seriously injured in the mishap. The young man whose parents owned the boat turned to his friends and said, "Don't worry, my parents will get me a new boat!"

Where do you suppose he got that attitude? It was developed and nurtured in him from the time he was an infant. Little things become big, with potentially devastating consequences if they go unchecked.

I knew if Tyler's response to the school rules went unchecked; if I failed to address his seemingly harmless attitude, right then and there, it would lead to further reactions of resistance and independence. My failure to act when this attitude was seemingly harmless would have opened the door to rebellious behavior later in his life. I was thankful to catch it in seed form and deal with it as an attitude before it grew to produce behavior that would be difficult to control or potentially devastating in its consequences.

Concluding Thoughts

Hurts and judgments from childhood prevent many adults from finding balance in the whole concept of discipline, and especially as it relates to spanking, time-outs, and grounding.

Many adults who were reared in a harsh, dominant, controlling environment that was physically and verbally abusive promise themselves that they will never treat their children as they were treated. This inner promise often results in an extreme type of parenting. At one end of the scale is a parent who struggles to administer discipline and ends up not disciplining at all. The result is behavior that is out-of-control in their children. On the other end of the scale are parents who abuse their children with hands or words, and who end up hating themselves for becoming just like their parents!

This kind of response is called an "inner vow," a personal promise formed from a judgment that lives in our hearts and works itself out in our lives. It is much like a computer virus, which corrupts the hard drive and contaminates files, altering the ability of the computer to operate properly. Inner vows do that to hearts and spirits. They prevent us from obeying God and keep us from implementing the truths that we have received. It will prevent you from finding the proper balance in your responses to your children.

To be free from an inner vow, you must forgive the person responsible for creating your pain, and you must renounce the vow of response that you have made, which is revealed in the form of statements like "I will never..." or "I will always..." This opens the door for you to ask God to forgive and heal you. Only then will you be able to properly train and correct your children.

It does not have to be an elaborate prayer. Just tell God you forgive those who hurt you and ask for His healing touch in your life. There is tremendous power in speaking out loud, and it is important that you hear yourself forgive them.

Next, ask God to do the work in your life to enable you to be an influential father or parent who properly understands and applies discipline to correct disobedient behavior. God will hear your prayer, and He will respond!

CHAPTER 9

Components of Balanced Discipline
Part 3—Accountability

Accountability simply adds wisdom, experience, and an objective perspective to the decision-making process, making it possible to avoid costly mistakes. It involves submitting to a limited number of individuals whose primary motivation involves your best interests and the fulfillment of God's will for your life.

Applying discipline without accountability is like buying a shiny new car and never checking the engine fluids once you leave the dealer's lot. Everything will work wonderfully for a while, but without oil, antifreeze, and hydraulic fluid, something will seize up, causing major damage, which could have easily been avoided! In the same way that a car needs oil, antifreeze, and hydraulic fluid to operate properly, discipline needs all three of its components—submission, correction, and accountability—to operate as God intended.

In the preceding two chapters, we have discussed submission to authority and corrective discipline. We will discuss in this chapter the final element, accountability. Accountability plays an important support role to the other two elements of discipline by protecting and reinforcing the lessons they teach. Without accountability, the instruction of discipline is quickly forgotten and its ability to influence and shape future behavior is lost.

What is Accountability?

Accountability is a term that evokes negative feelings from most men. Many men would define accountability as a relationship

Accountability is actually submission to an individual or small group based on a relationship of love and care.

between two individuals in which one person dominates or controls another. Real accountability, though, is not dominating or controlling at all. It is supportive and protective.

Accountability is actually *submission to an individual or small group based on a relationship of love and care.* A person who chooses to be accountable extends an open invitation to a select few people to influence his life, allowing them to review behavior and thoughts and give input or express concerns.

Accountability invites honest and caring input. Through relational care, accountability exposes blind spots and directs action away from harmful behavior or circumstances. It draws on another person's experience, wisdom, or knowledge of God and His ways to confirm direction, help fashion a well-thought-out strategy, or shape a response to weak areas of temptation.

Mechanisms of accountability establish a platform for mentoring. Mentoring is a process in which one person's knowledge and experience is used to shape and influence another for his or her benefit, not abuse. Accountability establishes a very important relationship between two individuals and must be treated with respect by both parties. The requirements to be effective as a mentor are the same requirements needed to be an effective father:

- A mentor should love God openly.
- A mentor should know and love you unconditionally.
- A mentor should earnestly desire to see God's will and blessing manifest in your life.

The most logical person to fulfill the duties of a mentor is a father. Who better? Who more qualified? It just makes sense that no person could be a better mentor to you than your father. Unfortunately, very few men have that type of relationship with their fathers. Most men do not have any real accountability in their lives. I know of some men who have sought accountability, but struggled in finding a man who had a clue about how to mentor them or what accountability was all about.

An accountability crisis has developed because we have been encouraged to be self-sufficient, producing an independence that has perverted the implementation of accountability among men. The lack of accountability among men today has produced devastating consequences in our personal lives as well as in our families.

God is always merciful to raise a voice of instruction when a truth or principle is ignored. The Promise Keepers ministry, founded by Coach Bill McCartney, was such a voice during the decade of the 90s— they became God's standard bearer to teach

> *Accountable relationships bless us by enabling us to make good decisions and preparing us to act right and lead our families in a healthy way.*

men the truth about accountability and call them out of independence and self-sufficiency.

Accountable relationships bless us by enabling us to make good decisions and preparing us to act right and lead our families in a healthy way. Unfortunately, most men have never seen or experienced accountability and have no idea about how to practice it with their children—and once again, a man can't transfer what he does not have.

How Does Accountability Work?

The purpose of accountability is to enable you to make wise decisions in your life. It begins with an attitude of submission, which, at its core, is a willingness to present issues for review or consideration before they are finalized or acted upon. The final decision is never the mentor's; it always remains with the individual who has to live with the outcome. Accountability simply adds wisdom, experience, and an objective perspective to the decision-making process, making it possible to avoid costly mistakes. It is not simply surrendering a decision on your circumstances to any random person you meet who might offer an opinion. It involves submitting to a limited number of individuals whose primary motivation involves your best interests and the fulfillment of God's will for your life.

Bad decisions result from several things: overwhelmingly strong desires, confusion caused by too many options, or "roller coaster" emotions that lead us through wide euphoric and depressive swings.

> *A mentor provides a stable, objective perspective to help sort out the confusion of emotions and desires.*

Accountability protects us from the influences that cause bad decisions. A mentor provides a stable, objective perspective to help sort out the confusion of emotions and desires. His input provides safety and produces the best possibility of success through the maze of life's options and varied circumstances.

Establishing the Foundation for Accountability

Accountability draws upon three qualities associated with humility: openness, honesty, and the ability to receive correction. Men have difficulty showing these important qualities because they think it makes them look weak, yet these traits are critical for accountability. I want to briefly discuss these three qualities.

The first quality is *openness*. No human can be present to monitor our thoughts and actions 24 hours a day, 7 days a week. So, we must be willing to openly discuss our thoughts, feelings, and behavior. We must be open with the issues that cause pressure or unrest and lead us to wrong behavior.

The second quality is *honesty*. We must be willing to truthfully explain our behavior and fully disclose, as much as we are aware, our reasons, thoughts, and intentions. Hiding feelings, issues, or behavior defeats the purpose and work of accountability.

The third quality is the ability to receive *correction*. Through the trust we have toward our mentors, we must be willing to allow them to confront us for misbehavior. We must listen and weigh carefully their objective perspective on the issues in our lives, factoring it into our actions. We cannot withdraw from correction by becoming defensive or angry. We must be able to rest in the trust we have in

> *You cannot mentor your children in accountable relationships until you have first made yourself accountable.*

our mentors, knowing that they are truly concerned with God's will and blessing for our life.

Accountability is as much an attitude as it is an action. Accountability is extended from one person to another whom they know, trust, and respect. It is done voluntarily not by force. We cannot be an effective mentor for our children until we first have made ourselves accountable. You should seek and embrace accountability for its benefits to your own life, but if that is not enough incentive, then do it for your children. Remember the principle of transference is the hub of all other parenting principles but especially the principle of accountability. Take action today to make sure that this principle is active in your life for the benefit of your children!

The Father's Role as Mentor

A mentor is not simply a good friend. A relationship of accountability deepens the friendship through a foundation of trust and molds the inner fabric of the person being mentored. While it is true that a friend can provide a listening ear, serve as a sounding board on issues, extend comfort, and offer free advice, a mentoring relationship goes much deeper. A mentor is trusted to give knowledgeable, loving advice, and to monitor behavior and attitudes throughout the circumstances of life. Trust enables the person being mentored to act on the mentor's advice in the immediate circumstance, whether it makes sense or not. This is not blind trust extended to a self-serving controlling person who is casually involved in your life; it is trust based on relationship that has no demands or strings attached. A mentor must make a significant, long-term commitment; he must draw on his experiences in life to guide the person under his care, not for his personal benefit, but for their best good.

A mentoring relationship with your children has its fullest expression as they mature. However, as with all aspects of parenting, you cannot wait to begin until they are approaching their adult years. Your work begins the day you bring them home from the hospital. A father cannot be a "pal-around" buddy with his child, as a friend might be: he is trainer, advisor, experienced liver of life, teaching his apprentice what he needs to know to succeed.

Until my dad passed away in 1989, he was a mentor to me. As a mentor he had influence upon every significant event in my life. I am fortunate to have enjoyed a similar relationship with my father-

> *Some men resist accountability because all they have experienced are dominating or controlling relationships. They have never experienced a relationship in which the input and advice were only meant for their good.*

in-law as well. Over the years, these mentors have given me wise counsel and saved me from many choices that would have brought certain disaster.

When I was elementary school age, my dad influenced me in a number of ways: through our involvement in athletics and YMCA Indian Guides, by his example in business and leisure, and especially in the way he treated my mom and my sisters. In my teen years, he taught me to drive, set parameters for dating, monitored my homework and school activities, and instilled important life values which were necessary for family and business success. As an adult, he has guided me in major purchase decisions, during career changes, and through other transitions of life.

My dad and my father-in-law met the three-fold requirement for a mentor that I mentioned above. They imparted wisdom and gave advice on all the significant decisions related to my life and family without dominating or controlling my behavior. Some men resist accountability because all they have experienced are dominating or controlling relationships. They have never experienced a relationship in which the input and advice were only meant for their good.

Because I have experienced this input from my dad and my father-in-law, I have had a model to use as a pattern for input to my children as they have matured. My dad was never controlling, manipulative or dominating, so my relationship with my children has never been that way either.

An Example of Accountability

When I became an adult, I made the conscious choice to continue to allow my dad to mentor me. It required an active decision on my part to be open, honest, and correctable. The result is that my dad protected me from costly mistakes that would have damaged my finances and my family.

One such incident took place in the first year of my marriage. We were living in our hometown of Omaha, Nebraska, in an apartment on a shoestring budget. I attended school and worked part-time. Jan was essentially the breadwinner, working full-time and providing the main financial support for our family.

One day, a good friend of mine offered to sell me his 1950 army surplus jeep, which had been sitting in storage for several years while he served in Vietnam. Although I was not a proficient mechanic, I had always had a dream of rebuilding a classic car. Of course, the jeep was not a classic car, but in my mind's eye, I could see it fully restored with a new paint job, super-charged engine, fancy wheels, a new interior, and a soft top. It was going to be *cool!*

At that moment, its condition was very rough. Although it had not been started in over two years, I remembered how it ran, and I could see in my imagination the smooth running power of the new 327-cubic inch engine I was going to put under the hood. It also did not look too great: its four coats of paint were peeling. Oh, there was one other minor problem—my friend could not find the key. But to me, that only added excitement to my feelings of anticipation. It meant the first step toward restoration was a new ignition switch!

Do I need to say that Jan did not share my enthusiasm? She had not yet caught the vision of what this ugly mass of metal was going to become. However, with a little persuasion, she saw the light and gave me her cautious okay to buy the jeep.

Since Jan and I lived in a rented apartment, my folks allowed me to use their garage for the project. The day was cold and rainy as Jan and I headed to my parents to eat supper before picking up my prize. After supper, my friend and I towed the jeep to my parents' house and pushed it into the garage. I was so proud of our work up to that point.

Jan came out for an inspection. She immediately burst into tears, and went running back into the house. It was worse than she had expected.

I was unfazed by her emotions. I knew she would come around as the restoration began to take shape. I was confident she would share my joy on the great day when we rolled my shiny hot rod, *the coolest jeep in the world,* out of garage for her maiden trip.

As I said good-bye to my friend, my dad came out for an inspection. Excited, I began to share my dream with him, describing in detail how I would restore this "beast" to glory. I felt that was a good manly type term to describe the beauty as she sat. Without a word, my dad circled the "beast," kicking the tires and inspecting the rust spots.

"So, what do you think, Dad?" I asked, certain he would share my excitement.

"Well, son," he said slowly, "you're an adult, and you're married, so this is between you and your wife. If you decide to do this, you are welcome to use the garage."

I needed more. I needed his encouragement and support. I wanted him to share the vision.

"Yeah, yeah, thanks Dad," I said, motioning with my arm, "But what do you *think*?"

And then my dad did something really great. *He told me the truth.*

A mentor must draw on his knowledge of God and his personal experience to offer counsel that will further God's purpose in his mentoree's life.

"What do I *think*?" he asked. "This is how I size up your situation, son...your wife is in the house crying, and this pile of junk is not a restoration project. It is a complete rebuild, a rolling sinkhole that will suck up dollars. Furthermore, what you are planning to do in restoring this worthless excuse for transportation will cost *big dollars*, which you don't have at this time in your life."

He paused, pondering his next statement, then continued. "You can do this if you want, but if you do, I am going to think you're stupid!"

Talk about a wet blanket on my vision!

I was blinded to the reality of my situation and needed a jolt back to reality. I needed the words of my mentor. Although my dad spoke sharply, I had learned from childhood to trust him; he was always interested in my success. His love for me propelled him to tell me the truth, and it opened my eyes to reality.

I sold the jeep the next day to a guy who worked at the plumbing supply house where I traded, and that ended my restoration project.

Many times, a mentor will see the facts clearly when you are blinded by circumstances as I was in this situation. My dad still respected my right to make the decision, but the strength of his view opened my eyes to the folly of my fantasy. I avoided a costly mistake, one that would have taken money we didn't have—but more importantly, he helped me avoid deeply damaging my relationship with Jan through selfish insensitivity. My attitude of submission to my dad allowed me to reap good results of accountability.

I learned principles of accountability as a child from my dad, which I carried on even as an adult, and in turn, I have taught them to my children. Todd, my oldest son, is now married with a family and a career. In 1999, when he had worked for the same employer for 5 years, another job opportunity came his way. He was offered a lucrative sales territory in a small West Texas town with a large pharmaceutical company. Within days of this unsolicited offer, his company offered him a transfer to a new assignment in New Zealand.

He struggled with what he should do—both opportunities had positive aspects and both had aspects that did not appeal to Todd and his wife. In the process of making his decision, he called on me as his father and his mentor and presented me with both opportunities. He openly discussed what he saw as the positives and negatives of both offers, and then he asked for my perspective and advice.

A mentor is not free to impose his will on the person he is in relationship with; he must draw on his knowledge of God and his personal experience, to offer counsel that will further God's purpose in his mentoree's life.

The father side of me wanted selfishly to advise his move to West Texas. It would have moved him just 3 hours from us and 2 hours from his wife's family. One offer would give him international business experience before he was thirty years old. The other offer would give him future promotion possibilities and good training but also it would put him in a small town in an out of the way place in West Texas.

As we talked, I felt the best offer for him and his future involved a move to New Zealand. He agreed but thought that it was a huge step for him and his young family. I assured him God would provide friends for them and establish them just as he would if they were relocating in the United States. With our encouragement and support, they moved to New Zealand.

It was God's plan for them and one of the best experiences of their life. It bolstered his business career, gave them a picture of God's power and work all across the world, and enabled them to make friends they will have for a lifetime. While they were there, they had their first child who now has duel citizenship in the United States and New Zealand.

Todd and his wife did not make the decision on their own, but with sensitive input from multiple mentors who confirmed God's work and His next step in their life. What a powerful blessing accountability is when it is understood in this way and works as I have described.

Concluding Thoughts

As a father, your decision to be accountable will bring blessing and protection to you and your family. If you need someone to be accountable to, ask God to help you find someone—a mentor who meets the three-fold requirement we have discussed. Your mentor might be a pastor, a Bible study leader, an older man in your life, a trusted friend, your father, or father-in-law.

Why not take action today, change your life, cast off independence, self-sufficiency, or pride? Submit your life to someone who cares for you, beginning with God; He is your best friend. He will bless your decision, bring you a mentor, and bring blessing and protection into your life. Your decision will also enable you to teach your children about accountability and prepare you to be a mentor to them, a benefit that will touch and influence generations.

CHAPTER 10

Using the Experiences of Life as Your Classroom

Children need to learn how to extract benefit from every circumstance before they leave home, so they can use this important skill throughout their adult life.

Most concepts essential for living as God designed are not learned through classroom instruction—things such as commitment, diligence, or honoring your word. My dad knew this, so he instilled these traits in us by encouraging us to use the situations of *life as our laboratory for application and discovery.*

I do not ever remember my dad teaching me his values through formal instruction. He might weave principles into our conversation at the dinner table, but the practical application of them was always taught and reinforced in the classroom of life. Even though we do not know what tomorrow will bring, parents can be assured that opportunities will develop on a daily basis to teach and impart God's principles for living to their children. Opportunities must be recognized and applied correctly for the training to have its maximum benefit.

When I was a boy, my dad modeled his values for me by allowing me to watch as he confronted everyday life situations applying his values to determine his response and shape the outcome. He also monitored my life and involved himself so he could identify circumstances that were impacting me and use them to show me how to use his principles to formulate my response to events. The focus of his concern was never the details of the circumstances; he was concerned with the principle to be imparted or the lesson to be learned. Using life's circumstances, he taught me to turn lemons into lemonade, making the most of the events by turning them into cases for study and instruction in the laboratory of life. In this way, he drove home such principles as commitment, diligence, and the priority of honoring my word.

The Correct View of Circumstances

As I have come to understand the sovereignty of God, I see His work expressed in the circumstances that arise in my life. This view has allowed me to recognize events for what they are, a time for God to teach me, an impartation of principles necessary to fulfill some aspect of His plan for my life.

He is always present, He is more powerful than any situation confronting me, and He has all knowledge so—no matter how challenging the events are to me—they are no challenge to Him.

> *He is always present; He is more powerful than any situation confronting me, and He has all knowledge, so— no matter how challenging the events are to me—they are no challenge to Him.*

This understanding of God's sovereignty has enabled me to view events and circumstances from the perspective of God's involvement in them and the ultimate good He is out to achieve.

It helps me to realize that every issue coming into my life must pass God's approval process; nothing is the result of bad luck, or under the control of entities seeking my harm. His sovereignty rules over every circumstance, casting a shadow of influence. So, when circumstances come my way that are difficult, unfair, or not what I desire, I trust in and am comforted by the knowledge that He is in control, and He has a plan that will even factor in the level of my experience to produce a good result (Romans 8:28). Not only will it produce a good result, He will use the situation to train and instruct me.

God promises to use the circumstances of our lives to accomplish His good work. Parents armed with this understanding, impart this perspective, through the principle of transference as they help their children deal with circumstances in their life. We must use circumstances to train and instruct them, thus building a framework for their understanding and accepting of God's work as it carries on throughout their whole life.

Using Circumstances to Instruct and

Impart Life Principles

Our two boys, Todd and Tyler, are six years apart. In their early years, Tyler was always Todd's "pesky" little brother. As they have matured, a friendship has developed that reflects a deep love and brotherly respect. However, during their years at home many situations provided teaching opportunities for me to impart lasting principles.

When Todd was about 16 and Tyler was 10, still in the "pesky" little brother stage, a situation occurred that exposed two flaws in the attitudes of my boys—giving me the opportunity to train them and impart my family values to them.

Todd's best friend, Kyle, called to invite Todd over to his house to "hang-out." When Tyler heard what his big brother was doing, he asked Jan and I if he could go with Todd to play with Kyle's younger brother, Collier. Kyle's family had four children like ours, and his younger brother, Collier, was Tyler's friend.

We gave our approval, over Todd's slight objection, discussed a time for them to come home, and off they went—Todd with his "pesky" little brother, Tyler, following behind.

When they returned from their visit, they walked in the house chatting away, in seemingly good moods. Everything about them seemed normal and positive. Then I noticed something out of the ordinary. Tyler's hair was wet. It was wet and neatly combed, as if he had just stepped out of the shower without time to dry it.

Both boys greeted Jan and I with a cheerful "hello" and headed to the kitchen for their evening feeding frenzy. I called them back and asked Tyler why his hair was wet.

"Oh *that*," he said, in as nonchalant a manner as he could muster. "I got a swirlie."

Now, I was an active boy as I grew up, and got into my share of mischief. But I was unfamiliar with the term "swirlie." Neither of the boys seemed to want to talk about it—I just couldn't tell if it was because they knew I was not going to like it, or because their bowls of ice cream were calling them from the kitchen. No matter, I made them stand there and explain a "swirlie" to me.

The boys explained that to give someone a "swirlie," you pick them up by their feet, hold them upside down, placing their head in the toilet as it is flushed. The water swirling around in the toiled bowl also "swirls" around the person's head drenching their hair, hence the name "swirlie."

The boys tried to convince me through their explanation that "swirlies" are a normal part of youthful entertainment, that everyone's doing it, and that it is a boy's right of passage into teenage coolness. After all, Tyler was going to be eleven years old soon, so it was natural that the older guys at Kyle's house would give him a premature induction into "teen-hood."

Their fast talking, positive spin, didn't fool me, I didn't buy it. It was an injustice to Tyler—*my son*—and I was *incensed*.

I asked Todd if he had participated in the prank, which immediately put him on the defense. He backpedaled, telling me that he did not take part in it, assuring me that Tyler had been a problem the whole night. To which I said, "You stood off and let them do this to your brother!" Still on the defense Todd said, "Dad, Tyler deserved it," as if that statement would get him off the hook and cinch my agreement with him.

Although I did not yell or become violent, I was noticeably upset. I turned and asked Tyler to follow me to the bedroom.

When we were alone, I asked Tyler how he felt about what had been done to him. At first, he maintained the party line, telling me everything was fine. Then, I pointedly asked him, "Weren't you embarrassed?" He said nothing.

"Are you frustrated…upset…do you feel violated?" I asked. Tears welled up in his eyes. And then the truth came out.

"Yeah, Dad," he said, his voice trailing off. "I *was* embarrassed, but they were bigger than me…"

His response was all that was needed for me to take action. I marched to the living room and instructed Todd that as a brother, he was never to allow someone to violate one of his siblings in this type of degrading manner. It made no difference if Tyler was a pest and "deserved it." The commitment of the family requires us to defend each other in times of need. *We can not allow someone else to bring inappropriate correction or to violate one of our family members.*

I went on to say that the kind of love that I expected between the members of our family was the kind of love that I modeled for

> *We cannot allow someone else to bring inappropriate correction or to violate one of our family members.*

them—a protective love with respectful measures of correction.

"I never want something like this to happen again," I told him. *"Do you understand?"*

All Todd could muster was a timid, breathy, *"Yes."*

I then loaded Tyler into my car and drove to Kyle's house. I wanted to confront the boys responsible for the prank.

I was controlled but firm. With carefully selected words, I told them that I did not approve of their behavior and I asked them to apologize to Tyler. They did.

There were two things about this prank that brought about such a strong reaction in me. First, I cannot stand activity or behavior that gains enjoyment at someone else's expense. Secondly, I also know that if your family will not defend you, no one will.

This situation exposed two flaws in the attitude of my boys. The first was a flaw in the way they found enjoyment. The second was a flaw in their commitment to family.

My reaction to this situation let the boys know that their behavior was not consistent with my values for our family. Without my correction and modeling of the appropriate action, this situation would have sent a message of passive approval to their behavior as an acceptable pattern for family relationships and entertainment— a pattern that not only would be transferred to my children, it would ultimately be passed on to theirs, simply because I reacted with the attitude that "boys will be boys."

Avoiding Extremes

Over the years, I have observed several extremes in the way parents' respond to situations that impact their children. In order to take advantage of situations, using them for training and instruction, we must avoid the extremes as we walk with our children through their situations.

1. The over-nurturing response The first extreme is a response of over-nurturing and over-protecting by the parent. This occurs when parents allow the love they have for their children to overpower their responsibility to train, prepare, and protect them. The result is that they shield their children from the lessons of life that are to be learned from trying circumstances by coming to their defense or fighting their battles.

Clayton was a tall strong man with a deep intimidating voice. Most of the children stayed away from him when he was out in his yard. Clayton Jr. was big for his age and looked like he would follow his father's pattern for size. However, Clayton Jr. was a wimp. He was teased or picked on by nearly every child in the neighborhood. Often the teasing became so mean-spirited that it brought Clayton to tears. This treatment of his son infuriated Clayton Sr.; when it happened he would single out kids in the neighborhood whom he felt had spearheaded the attack and yell at them. On several occasions he marched over to the child's house and gave the parents of the offending child a very colorful piece of his mind.

However, his actions did not change the situation for his son. Rather than teach his son how to react in this type of adversity he came to his defense, fighting his battle for him. The result was a view among the kids and many of the parents that Clayton Sr. was a grumpy, mean man. The response of his father increased disrespect for Clayton Jr. among his peers, and produced an inability for him to stand up for himself in the face of teasing. He never learned how to stand and confront anything apart from his dad doing it for him.

Clayton and his family moved when he was in high school, but until the time they moved, the situation had not changed for

Clayton Jr. Even in high school his dad fought his battles for him, perpetuating a weakness in adversity and a personality of insecurity. By fighting our children's battles for them, we produce weak and dependent children who lack the necessary skills for life and the ability to solve problems for themselves. Their weaknesses follow them right into adulthood where they face even more critical battles.

Parents *should* respond to their children's tough situations with loving care and sensitivity that is positive and healthy. However, a caring parent should not shield his children from every unjust situation. As a rule of thumb, I have stepped in when the situation posed physical or emotional danger, or when the age difference of those involved put my children at a disadvantage in the situation. However, I am always careful not to involve myself in a way that obstructs the training benefit of the circumstance.

2. The detached response A second extreme is that of detachment. Detachment results when parents withdraw from personal intervention in their children's problems based on the thought that the children will "fully benefit" only when dealing with the situation on their own. Detached parents fear that the force of their personality might inappropriately determine a solution for their children. So they withdraw from the circumstances to force their children to determine a solution on their own.

Their detachment leaves their children to deal with something for which they are not yet prepared. By contrast, children will grow in self-esteem and confidence, as they respond to life's situations *under the scrutiny of a caring parent.*

A response of withdrawal is especially unproductive when the children have not reached the appropriate development level to be able to handle the situation. Children cannot be the judge of their own maturity level, so when they lack the relational or emotional development to know how to respond, a parent must step in to help them walk through the situation.

When Todd was 4 years old, we lived between two families with boys his age. It was wonderful to have friends for our son to play with on the same side of the street within 100 feet of our front door. The three boys were good friends and playmates, but often they would fight over the same toy. Sometimes two of the boys would join together to form alliances against the other boy, and feelings or bodies would get hurt. The mom's were usually the referee being called in to settle the disputes that arose among the boys.

One day Jan told me that the mom's of all the boys had decided not to referee any longer, instead they would send the tattling boy back to the other two and make them work it out amongst themselves. It sounded like a good solution to me as it would force them to learn to solve their disputes and get along with each other. I agreed to support the decision if I was around when a dispute broke out.

All appeared to be working the first few weeks after implementing the new strategy. The boys were still fighting, but they were forced to work it out and the mom's were less stressed by the tattling of the boys. One evening I walked in from work to the wailing of one of the boys as he stomped out of the bedroom area of our house. He was crying and screaming emphatically that he would never play with Todd again. As he stomped by me, I attempted to stop him to find out what had happened. My wife got my attention and reminded me that we had agreed not to involve ourselves in the boy's disputes. So, I let him go by me, crying and screaming out the front door on the way to his house. If the pattern held true all would blow over by the morning and he would be back over to play. However, he did not come over the next day and neither did the other boy.

When I arrived home the next night from work Jan was mortified. One of the neighbors came down to tell us that Todd's little friend had broken his collarbone in the scuffle the boys had over a plastic golf club the previous day. As the boys wrestled for control of the club, Charlie lost the scuffle and fell into the doorknob. His crying departure the previous day was more than a disagreement between the boys. When we learned what had happened we immediately went to the parents and expressed our sorrow. We offered to pay their medical expenses. They were cool but polite and refused our offer. We asked if there was anything we could do and they thanked us but said no.

Over the next couple of days the mother's of Todd's two friends got together and decided that Todd was mostly at fault and that he was more aggressive than their son's, posing a danger to their well being. Together they decided to not let their sons play with Todd any longer. Over the next several months we tried everything we knew to make amends for the situation but the parents were resolute in their conviction that Todd posed a danger to their boys.

Day after day Todd would sit on his big wheel or stand at the front door and watch as the two boys drove from house to house, passing right by our driveway. As they went by Todd they would chant, "We can't play with you, you're mean."

It broke our heart to watch the disappointment on our son's face. His four year old mind did not understand why the boys would no longer play with him. Finally, having tried everything we could think of to resolve the issue, God opened a door for us to move.

As parents, we had removed ourselves too far from their situation and the consequences were not good for the boys or us. It was the most emotionally and financially draining thing to impact

Parents must maintain open lines of communication with their children through all the stages of their development to know and understand the problems they're confronting.

our son and us in the early years of our family.

Parents must maintain open lines of communication with their children through all the stages of their development to know and understand the problems they're confronting. Each stage has unique challenges that must be overcome. When the children are in the preschool years, it is easy to cut off communication because of their seemingly constant tattling on each other. However, to listen does not necessarily foster tattling as some may fear. Instead, it enables an evaluation of the situation and a determination of the children's ability to respond in an appropriate way. At preschool ages, each situation requires some level of parental evaluation to determine the emotional and physical demands the situation places on the children, along with an assessment of the maturity level needed to respond properly. It is our responsibility to make sure our children are not out-manned physically or numerically as they respond to situations.

Finally, we must monitor the outside factors working in the situation to make sure our children will not be overwhelmed as they work out a solution. By outside factors I mean things such as older children, who may use their size or experience to take advantage, or when another parent has become involved in the situation. When one parent steps into the situation, both child's parents should become involved to provide balance and protection. Parental concerns must be addressed parent-to-parent to determine a helpful strategy that will benefit all involved in the situation.

By parental involvement and balance I do not mean that another parent is forbidden from correcting my children without my involvement. If my children are misbehaving and they are under the care of another adult, I want that adult to correct my children. However, when my children do not respond to the correction of that adult, or when their behavior requires discipline beyond a time-out, I want to be involved.

3. The controlling response This occurs when parents attempt to control the future or directional decisions of their children, or the circumstances surrounding their children, to make sure everything is fair and right, shaded properly, and no one has an unfair advantage. Controlling parents use their wealth, social position, physical dominance, or their authority to determine an outcome in situations involving their children.

In doing so, controlling parents create an artificial environment for their children, one that shields them from the consequences of their behavior or makes them dependent for the purpose of directing their life. Controlling parents see their responses as a protective shield for their children, but it ultimately builds a defiant attitude of disrespect in their children as they attempt to break free from their parents' control.

Eric and Judy are loving parents that have been involved in the activities of their children from preschool age and continue to be involved with their children who are now adults. When their middle child, Susan, graduated from college they were there to celebrate. They helped her move to a new city to begin her career and were quite opinionated about where she should live. They thought an apartment complex that was gated with on-site security was where she needed to live, but there were not many young singles who lived in the complex and the rent was more than their daughter wanted to pay. On the other hand, Susan knew the complex she wanted. It was newly constructed and very popular with singles just beginning their careers. Her parents insisted that she live in the complex they felt best and offered to pay the monthly difference so their daughter could live in safety. When Susan declined their offer, they were upset and used every conversation leading up to her move and after she occupied her new apartment to restate their concerns. On one occasion Judy sent clippings from the newspaper of burglaries in her area and one in her complex. They would not let the issue go away. Their attempt to control their daughter strained their relationship with her and although she never completely rebelled against her parents' values, she did distance herself from them and their relationship suffered as a result.

Another reaction children make to controlling parents is to comply under their control. It may look good from a distance but this unhealthy dependence by the children upon their parents actually weakens their ability to deal with people or issues often turning the children into relational "brats" who are unable to cope with any circumstance that does not conclude to their benefit.

Tim's parents controlled every aspect of his life. As a young single adult his parents had final say on where he lived, the car he drove, and even whom he dated. Although Tim was living on his own and was several years into his work career, his parents dominated his life.

Tim made no decision without discussing it with them first and receiving their approval. He had learned that if he had their support in his decisions then they would bail him out if he got in trouble; but if he took action without their approval he was on his own.

Tim struggled with making and keeping friends and finding a girlfriend who would put up with the control his parents exerted in his life. As a result, he was lonely and was very underdeveloped in his social skills. Tim's dependence upon his parents had stunted his growth as an adult and made him unable to stand on his own. Rather than providing encouragement and counsel to help him while still allowing him to make his own decisions his parents controled his life in an unhealthy way.

These extremes keep our children from developing into stable balanced adults.

Let me explain the difference between correction and control. When I observe behavior in my children that is inconsistent with my standard of values, I correct their behavior. I expect a change, and if I do not see a change, discipline is initiated. Correction is a response to the child and his behavior. Control is an attempt to

Your good intentions or concern for your children do not justify any attempt to control them or the circumstances of their lives.

manipulate circumstances and the people involved in the circumstances toward a determined outcome. When children are young and while they live in our home, it is appropriate to exert some control over their life. But even then we must be careful not to build a pattern of dependent control between our children and ourselves.

When they leave our home to establish a life of their own we must assume the role of advisor. Our good intentions or concern for our children does not justify any attempt to control them or the circumstances of their life. Controlling responses by us instills weakness in our children. It also erects barriers of resistance that can damage and even destroy the relationship we have with our children.

The goal of good parenting is to avoid extremes in responses, to find a balance that protects children as they deal with circumstances, but also allows the children to gain experience and training that prepares them for life. We must protect our children from unfair situations while extracting from the circumstances the fullest instructional value.

Parents must learn when to lend assistance to their children, when to come to their defense, how to support them, yet allow them to stand up and fight for themselves. We must learn when and how to use circumstances for their highest instructional purpose. Finding balance in situations affecting our children takes proactive effort, and diligent sensitivity, to ensure we do not lose the instructive benefit of the situation. Our children need to learn how to extract benefit from every circumstance before they leave home, so they can use this important skill throughout their adult life.

Concluding Thoughts

Jesus taught and modeled the principle of transference to his disciples. He told them the student is not above the teacher, that the students will learn what the teacher has experienced. Do you see God in the circumstances of your life? Is He recognized and included in the situations that arise in your business, pleasure, and family?

It is critical to develop an awareness of God's involvement in every situation so you can gain an understanding on how to partner with Him as He works. An awareness of God's work, and your partnership with Him, will maximize the learning benefit in each situation.

Finally, has God been convicting your heart throughout this chapter? Perhaps you have slid to an extreme in the way you respond to the circumstances that impact your children? If so, take some steps to move away from the extreme to a place of balance. To do so will require you to respond to some things in your own life. This might include forgiving your parents for being controlling or for being detached in their response to your situations.

I encourage you to take the steps necessary to forgive others, and to renounce vows and judgments you have made in response to the hurts or frustrations of your own life. Unforgiveness, vows, and judgments will keep you from finding the place of balance, and prevent you from being the father of influence that is God's design.

CHAPTER 11

The Importance of Spending Time with Your Kids

"Children's children are the crown of old men, And the glory of children is their father."

Proverbs 17:6

Special memories enjoyed with our children are the result of accumulated times of mundane activities, committed work, and patient efforts to build understanding and communication. What great joy there is when it all comes together in a finished product.

The average father spends less than five minutes each day with his children. When I first heard this statistic, I dismissed it as absurd. I thought of all our family activities, and how often I involved myself in activities with my children. I concluded that the report must be in error. However, as I have interacted with other men, I have become convinced the statement is true, at least as it relates to the quality of time fathers give to their children. I have become aware that most of the time, fathers spend with their children is not quality time. Like the saying: "The lights are on, but no one is home,"—it seems that when fathers are with their children, they are present in body, but distracted by thoughts of work or other concerns. Their lights are on, but no one is home!

I believe there are two major reasons men are distracted and disconnected from their children. First, men usually work in an ordered environment, subject to time schedules and deadlines. The home environment is often just the opposite—chaotic and disjointed. Children are naturally active and bring a certain amount of disorder to the home. This sense of chaos is compounded if the children are undisciplined, loud, demanding, selfish, and out of control, which all children are to some degree. Children naturally behave this way; it is a part of their foolish nature and it changes very little as they mature into their teen years.

If children are not trained, their undisciplined, out of control, behavior will follow them right into adulthood. Proactive parenting, the kind that is involved and focused, is needed to train children how to act.

The chaos and disjointed atmosphere that often surrounds the kids can lead a father to detach himself emotionally from his children when they are young; once he has disconnected, he will most often remain that way through every stage of their development.

The second reason men's attentions are turned away from their children is because of the demands placed on them by their careers or their involvement in a wide variety of personal interests. Men often find it difficult to balance family time with a full slate of work responsibilities and the demands from friends, hobbies, civic clubs and other similar interests. After working hard, it is easy for a man to justify a selfish focus centered on his needs and to reward himself with activities that offer personal gratification and excitement. With that type of competition for undivided attention, it is easy to understand—*although it doesn't make it right*—why men end up distracted and unfocused toward their children, spending their free time other places. Children are the most demanding and least gratifying of their choices.

We often make shortsighted decisions because it is difficult for us to consider the long-term benefits of sacrificial investment in the lives of our children. We perpetuate our insensitivity with the deceptive thought that we *can* make it all work, not recognizing that we have given the best of our time and emotions somewhere else— and that leaves us with nothing to give to our children. Deep down we know we cannot do it all, but it is difficult to make the tough decisions that put priorities in their right place. The price we pay is in missed opportunities to train and influence our children.

Using the Opportunity of Time

Most men savor great moments in sports. What man wouldn't have wanted to be present to watch Joe Frazier upset Mohammad Ali for the heavyweight boxing title? Or to see the American hockey team beat the Russians in the Olympics for the gold medal? Great moments—the ones that are remembered with meaning—are best enjoyed when they are experienced firsthand. Highlights and reruns do not compare. To fully experience the thrill of the event, one must be there when it happens. It's as simple as that.

If we could easily predict a great moment, we could arrange our schedules so that we could be there to experience it firsthand. Instead, it takes sacrifice, priority, and commitment to create opportunities that make it possible to witness great moments. This is true with sporting events as well as great moments with our

> *It takes sacrifice, priority, and commitment to create opportunities that make it possible to witness great moments.*

children. A father's presence is a catalyst for producing great moments, ones that develop meaningful memories with his children.

Absentee and distracted fathers miss the greatest moments in their children's lives, only experiencing them in "highlights" or "reruns." I remember watching my son score the winning soccer goal for his team, meeting my daughter's first date, watching my children learn to swim, helping them with their homework, and witnessing a thousand other significant events in their lives. I have never regretted sacrificing the time.

As my children have grown to be adults, my perspective of their childhood has changed. I realized too slowly the shortness of their time in our home. When they were young, their college years and beyond seemed an eternity away. The year our oldest son graduated from high school was when this first hit me. I saw how quickly he had grown up, and I regretted not spending more quality time with him. There was so much more I wanted to share with him to be sure he was prepared for adult responsibilities and opportunities. There was so much more I wanted to teach him. It seemed as though I blinked my eyes, and he was headed off to college. I determined right then and there that I would make a change to ensure I did not repeat this mistake with our remaining children. I also went back and invested in his life in a greater way.

I sat down one morning to write down the subjects I wished I had covered with Todd more completely. I quickly came up with a dozen subjects I wanted to cover and explain in greater depth to make sure he had a solid basis of understanding for things he would encounter as an adult.

They were subjects like the most essential quality to look for in a wife, the most important principle in financial management, what really makes a person successful, etc. These were subjects that we had talked about many times, but I was insecure in the thoroughness of my training.

So I decided I would write him a weekly email and present to him my thoughts and perspective on these important subjects. Through the beauty of email communication, he could print off my thoughts for consideration at a convenient time and then respond back to me with his comments or questions.

I felt it was the second best thing to face-to-face communication. I borrowed the format from Josh McDowell, the Campus Crusade for Christ leader, teacher, and author. He actually wrote love letters to his son and daughter while they were in college. His letters became the text for two of his books. The format was loving and interactive rather than stuffy and preachy. Before I started sending them, I told Todd what I was going to do and why. He happily received my input because he knew my motive was love for him.

I also made a decision to establish personal times with each of our other 3 children to give greater opportunity for a memorable moment. One way I have accomplished this is to treat each of my children to breakfast or lunch regularly. I began having a weekly lunch with Lisa, our oldest daughter and second child, during her senior year of high school. We had a time each week for just the two of us to be together. There was no specific agenda. We would simply talk about whatever might come up in the conversation, or express feelings or thoughts from the day, or talk about an event from the morning or one coming later in the day. When Tyler, our third child, became a senior, I continued the weekly lunch with him. These lunch times have produced special memories with both Tyler and Lisa.

I decided not to wait until Lindsay's senior year to share one-on-one time with her. We ate breakfast together at least once a week. I got the full load of joy, concerns, and information from our most expressive child. These times with my children have produced great moments, priceless memories worth more than great riches. The special times we have shared will be relived and enjoyed between us, over and over, in the years ahead.

In addition, I have sought to communicate to my children that they always have priority in my life—at home and at work. My assistant knows that I am always available to my children, by telephone and in person. My instructions are that if my children need me, *I am to be interrupted.* When my children come in or call me at work, I am not concerned about my pressing responsibilities or my children's insensitivity to my business. Rather, I am concerned that I communicate at all times my love and care for my children. I have taught them to be respectful of people and of my schedule while demonstrating to them in real terms that they come first.

This concept did not originate with me; it is my Heavenly

> *To teach my children to understand God's love and care, I must mirror God's actions as best I can.*

Father's. It is how He responds to me. He is always available to listen to my concerns, comfort my emotions, and provide for my needs. He is never too busy for me. To teach my children to understand God's love and care, I must mirror God's actions as best I can. My dad showed me the way.

When I was in my last semester before college graduation, I was in the process of interviewing for a job. One evening Jan and I went over to my parent's house for dinner. My dad and I were sitting in the den talking as we waited to be called to the table.

He reached into his pocket and handed me his business card. On the back of the card he had written this brief message, "I am your best friend and I will always be your best friend, if you ever need me call, no matter when, where, or what time it is…Love, Dad." That was the most important gift I received for my college graduation and in a monetary sense it was the least expensive. In fact it is the only gift I received that I can still remember today. I carried that card in my billfold until several years after my dad passed away, occasionally I would take it out and re-read the message. What a gift from my dad!

I have found that you can never recapture the important opportunity created by a crisis of concern, an emotional trauma, or a pressing need. A kind word, a gentle touch, or solving a critical problem at the moment of need creates impressions in our children's minds that they will never forget.

Developing a Long Term Perspective

Today, the virtues of self-sacrifice and delayed gratification are not widely taught or embraced. Most of us have been persuaded to think only about ourselves and only for the moment. We do not want to wait until tomorrow, next week, next month, or next year. If we want something, we want it now. As these two important virtues have slipped away from our behavior, they have taken with them an appreciation for the value of our time. Our time has value, and we should invest it with thoughtful consideration to achieve the maximum return.

To produce a great return on the investment we make in our children, it helps to think in financial terms. The value of our time can easily be converted into a dollar value so that the investment we make can be evaluated like any other financial investment opportunity. For example, consider a man with an annual income of $36,000. If he works 5 days a week, 40-hours a week, with 2 weeks of vacation a year, he will work 2,000 hours during the calendar year. By dividing the hours into his salary, his annual income is converted into a value of $18 per hour. We can now use the hourly rate to convert a favorite activity into its cost in time: a round of golf that takes four hours of time converts into a cost of $72 in time on top of the green fees, a new bass/ski boat used every weekend might convert into a half-year or more of time dollars on top of the purchase price and operating cost of the boat itself.

When we include in our thinking the cost of our time, along with the cost of the purchase, we become aware of the total costs associated with the item we desire. The physical and mental costs associated with our work have a clearly defined dollar value. Following this process more often, as we evaluate the need and timing of a purchase, would help us properly prioritize it by considering the investment of our time.

Spending time with our children should be viewed as any investment for the future. For example, most employees participate in a retirement plan in which they can invest a certain amount of money each pay period. The theory is that a small amount invested regularly over a long period of time can accumulate into a large amount through the miracle of compound interest. When preparing for retirement, it is wisest to begin early in your life and

...even if the amount of time you invest is not as large as you would like, your investment in your children will compound into a tremendous treasure.

invest small amounts that will have a long time to grow, rather than waiting until you can invest large amounts later in life because you lose the benefit of compounding interest.

Similarly, if you begin when your children are young and invest consistent amounts of time, even if the amount you invest is not as large as you would like, your investment in your children will compound into a tremendous treasure. The amount you invest today may seem insignificant, but it compounds to produce a great return.

I know a man who is by most every measure a man of great success. He has overcome obstacles to become a huge success in his career. Through his business success, he has also achieved great financial wealth as well.

However he has paid a great price for his success: he is never home or available for his children. He has missed most of his children's big events. He has not been there to see their sport success, be there for their awards banquets, or see their recitals. He has provided them with a comfortable lifestyle and there is no doubt he loves his children. The pattern of his response started when his children were young and has continued into their adult life.

When his oldest son got caught with drugs in his car he was not there to deal with the situation; he was on a business trip. When another son was honored at his company's annual awards banquet by being inducted into the presidents counsel of young leaders, he wasn't there. Even though he was notified before hand of his son's award, he could not (or did not) rearrange his schedule to be there to share in this important event in his son's life.

I don't know the thinking of this father, but I do know the effect, possibly he was detached and insensitive to the opportunity he missed. Or maybe he is acting toward his son just like his dad responded to him. Possibly he is thinking he will wait until a better time—comforting himself with the false idea that at some future time he will make up for his absence. Often that time never comes or when it does his son will have built a life that has no room for sharing the important moments with him.

Regardless of his thinking, this I know—every father, even a very busy father must invest time in small increments, at important moments, and in mundane circumstances, declaring to his children they are an important priority in his life. It cannot be put off until a better time because there may not be one.

The Benefits of an Investment Strategy

Over the years, I have invested time in my children. I have memories of wonderful events, and today I am enjoying the benefits of my investment strategy.

Let me share a return that I received on the investment I made in my oldest son. My life is rich with examples like this one from each of my children—the result of compound interest that has accrued on the investment I have made of my time.

On December 30, 1995, Todd married a wonderful young woman. Days before the wedding, we celebrated Christmas with our daughter-in-law-to-be for the first time. It was an exciting and emotional celebration, a time of significant change in our family. When the time arrived for me to open my gift from Todd, he presented me with a package that was about the size of a shirt box. I shook it and could not imagine what it could be. It was much heavier than a shirt.

I tore away the wrapping paper and discovered a picture frame. Mounted in the frame was a poem, neatly printed and matted.

Todd said he had written the poem for me as he thought about the step he was taking into marriage. He said I had taught him so many things—things that he wanted to pass on to his children— and he wanted to express his appreciation with words. I could not contain my emotion as I read. I want to share his poem with you:

Lessons of a Father
By Todd Lane

To learn how to fly with a gentle nudge,
    To learn to forgive and not hold a grudge.
To know how to talk with a bridled tongue,
    To know how to walk and lead the young.
To follow the advice and counsel of peers,
    To follow God's Word will enhance your years.
To give with a heart that feels better when done,
    To give with the love of God for His Son.
To know it's all right for a man to cry,
    To know it will hurt when we say good-bye.
To love and live an enjoyable life,
    To love my family and honor my wife.
To see the good in a ridiculous mess,
    To see that my children have a place to rest.
To never give reason to question your word,

To never let anger from your mouth be heard.
To learn to encourage with a simple smile,
To learn that the best go the extra mile.
I pattern my life after the lessons I've learned,
The teaching goes on, but now it's my turn.
I go with strength from the training I've had,
These are the things I've learned from my dad.

Concluding Thoughts

I can truthfully say that the time Jan and I have invested in each of our four children has been the best investment we ever made—the most rewarding and the most profitable. It has returned to us far more than we could have ever imagined!

How are you investing your time? Are you prioritizing a portion of your time for your children? Or, are you waiting for the day when you can make a big deposit of time and missing the compounding benefits of a little invested on a regular basis?

I once heard this description of what it is like to work for the telephone company: *some days you dig holes, some days you plant poles, some days you string wire, and some days you make a connection.* Without the holes, poles, and wire, there will not be a connection. Special memories enjoyed with our children are the result of consistent times of mundane activities, committed work, and patient efforts to build understanding and communication. What great joy there is when it all comes together in a finished product.

It is not too late for you to dig holes, plant poles, and string wire. It's not too late to make investment deposits in your children's lives. Your children may even be adults now, with children of their own. Don't worry, there is still time. Your effort and the investment of your time will bring awesome rewards.

CHAPTER 12

The Balance of Two Perspectives

"Who can find a virtuous wife?
For her worth is far above rubies.
The heart of her husband safely trusts her;
so he will have no lack of gain."

Proverbs 31:10-11

My wife, Jan, increases my effectiveness as a father. Her support, insight, and perspective minimizes my weaknesses and compounds my strengths.

King Solomon, possibly the richest king in the history of the world, certainly considered to be one of the wisest men in the history of the world, made a simple yet profound statement. "*Two are better than one...,*" he said, "*For if they fall, one will lift up his companion.*" (Ecclesiastes 4:9-10)

This statement is true in business relationships as well as in marriage. My wife, Jan, increases my effectiveness as a father. Her support, insight, and perspectives minimize my weaknesses and compound my strengths. We are partners working together to rear our children.

Over the years, as I have counseled married couples, newlyweds, and engaged couples, I have been struck by the way God designed the mechanism of attraction between a man and a woman. The relationship often begins with a physical attraction, only to continue if both people have common life goals, dreams, and interests. Once this important foundation is in place, there is diversity in just about every other facet of their life. A quiet person tends to attract an outgoing and gregarious one. A high-strung, opinionated person attracts an easy-going, "whatever" type, and so on.

My wife and I are that way. She is fun-loving, spontaneous, and talkative. I tend to be more organized, less spontaneous, and more introspective. Together, we share a common intensity related to our commitment to God. We passionately desire to love and serve Him. In most other ways, Jan and I are different from each other.

I write this as encouragement for you so that you will embrace and respect the differences in your wife. As a good friend of mine says, "If you're both the same, one of you is unnecessary." Those differences attracted you to her in the first place.

I am embarrassed to say that for too many years of my marriage, my constant effort was to mold my wife into my image. When we differed, I would try to help her get the "right" perspective. I "knew" my way was always better than hers and was confident it was the "right" way to respond. I rarely, if ever, gave Jan credit for having a beneficial perspective—unless it lined up with mine. When children arrived in our home, parenting revealed new differences in our perspectives.

Who is right? Is one way better than another? The male ego wants to dictate the response to circumstances, and in doing so, works against any perspective that is not its own. But, in reality, the variety of experience produces a perspective that brings new insights and options to any situation.

> *...rather than try to change your wife, seek to understand her, and embrace her uniqueness.*

So, rather than try to change your wife into your likeness, seek to understand her, and embrace her uniqueness, by accepting and celebrating the way she is different from you. By doing so, you will allow her perspective to minimize your weaknesses and add to your strengths.

Differences Add Strength

Over the years, as Jan and I have come to embrace each other's differences, we have realized a great advantage in our parenting. Our children know that if they want cake, candy, or pop between meals, they had better ask me, not their mom. If they want compassion for forgetting a responsibility, they know to go to their mom not me.

How do our children figure these things out? They are not concerned with ego, authority structure, or roles of responsibility; our children are simply attempting to get what they want! Over time, they learn the easiest and most successful route. When parents become occupied with trying to change each other, they find themselves in constant competition, and miss bringing the power and strength of unity into their relationship.

As we honestly examine our personality and its influence on our behavior, we can admit our weaknesses and lean on our partner's strength. Even when your wife is not strong in your area of weakness, you can maximize your results by trusting that two heads are better than one. A unified decision will always accomplish more than a decision based on individual perspective.

Keys to Unified Decisions

1. <u>Never be pressured into a decision</u>. As a parent, always keep in mind that you are in charge. You do not have to make decisions under pressure.

Children apply pressure in order to get a decision they want. They often present an issue with unrealistic time constraints. They ask for a decision immediately. *This is a once-in-a-lifetime opportunity,* they often say, *and we have to decide right now!* Our rule of thumb in pressure situations, where time does not allow full consideration of the details, is to say "no." Some requests can be decided upon quickly; others need careful consideration and discussion.

Children need to learn patience and gain an understanding that God's plan will succeed regardless of timeframe or circumstances. Making hurried decisions is one of the best ways to miss God's plan. If the opportunity is right, careful consideration and discussion will produce the response they desire, and confirm God's hand in the process. If some good opportunities are missed in the process, it will not be the end of the world. More bad opportunities will be avoided than good ones missed.

2. <u>Never undermine your partner</u>. All children are born with an innate ability to manipulate. When children do not receive the response they want from one parent, they will often attempt an "end-run" appeal with the other parent. An "end-run" usually

involves some deceit on our children's part. Somehow, they fail to disclose the already communicated decision as they make their request to the parent being manipulated.

On those few occasions where they do reveal the decision made by the other parent, it is to benefit their appeal of the decision as being unfair, lacking real understanding of the circumstances, or as being totally uncompassionate! Regardless of the method, children can argue pretty convincingly, sometimes generating anger and judgment toward our spouse for their "unfair, harsh, or shallow" response to a "wonderful" child. *Be careful of this attempt to divide and conquer!*

Jan and I respond to situations like these by supporting each other's decision, even if we disagree. If either of us feels the decision was in error, we discuss it behind closed doors without our children's knowledge. If we need to make a change, the one that *originally made the decision communicates the change* to the children, along with the reasons for change.

3. Tag team using each other's strengths to make the best decisions. If we allow pride or ego to stand in the way of our ability to join our strengths and cover our weaknesses, we miss the opportunity to arrive at the best solutions. A husband and wife must lean on each other, even deferring to one another in the decision-making process.

When Todd entered junior high, he came home one day excited about a school dance scheduled for the coming weekend. He wanted to go and could hardly wait.

Jan was dead set against him going, and because she is more outgoing and party loving than I am, she had better insight into the pressures and temptations that Todd would encounter during and after the dance with his friends. She thought he was too young to be exposed to those pressures and temptations.

I felt he should be allowed to go—with clearly defined parameters. The dance would provide a good training vehicle for our maturing son. Jan had strong reservations, but she listened to my position, and we worked together to reach a decision we both could accept. Together, we created a safe and fun experience for

Todd and one that allowed us to watch and participate in his experience. We agreed to be parent chaperons at the dance. That way he got to experience the dance and we got to monitor his experience.

4. <u>If you are divorced, put aside personal disagreements with your ex-spouse and work together for the benefit of your children</u>. Over half of all marriages are now dissolved through divorce, and most of those marriages have produced children.

> *...set aside the animosity and hurts associated with your relationship and continue to balance your perspectives for the blessing and benefit of your children.*

Divorce often has a negative impact on a man's interest and ability to remain involved with his children. If you are a divorced parent you must set aside the animosity and hurts associated with your relationship and continue to balance your perspectives through a parenting partnership for the blessing and benefit of your children. You can still create a legacy for and in your kids, even if it didn't work in your marriage.

To do this, you must communicate with each other the issues of your concern related to the children. Also, you must agree to support each other's authority during conversations with your children. When you disagree with each other, do so privately, away from the children, in a place where it will not be overheard.

If you or your ex-spouse have remarried, do not allow disagreement or conflict with the new spouse to enter into your parenting partnership. You and your ex-spouse are the parents, but through remarriage, secondary partners have been introduced into the parenting process. Agree to work with your ex-spouse's new partner to benefit the children.

Recently released data confirms that children never want their parents to separate or divorce. If you are divorced, I urge you to make a commitment to set aside unresolved issues for the benefit of your children, no matter how overwhelming the task may seem. Working together, you can bring security and blessing to your children even though it is too late to restore your marriage.

Concluding Thoughts

I have been relating many of my experiences as a father in the chapters of this book. However, it is not my influence alone that has produced great children. My influence on my children would have been less effective without the partnership of my wife. Her support, insight, and perspective have minimized my weaknesses and solidified my strengths. As I conclude this chapter, I leave you with some questions to consider:

Have you expressed your appreciation to your wife for the contribution she has made to your children's development and to your parental success? Have you fully appreciated the unique qualities and individual strengths that your wife contributes to your marriage and family?

Take a minute to thank God for the gift He has given you in the person of your wife. Then, be sure to follow that prayer of thanksgiving with a verbal expression of thanks to her. Why not make renewed commitments to capitalize on each other's strengths as you parent your children? A decision to do that will greatly enhance your influence as a father.

CHAPTER 13

Preparing Your Child for His Destiny

*Each of our children are different.
They are unique in personalities, abilities,
talents, and interests. To find their destiny,
they cannot be shoved into the same mold
or left to self-develop.*

Destiny is a lofty ideal to be considered, for the thought of it includes the idea of ultimate purpose, plan, and fortune—a predetermined course of events. The place to begin for those who desire to fulfill their purpose in life is with the thought that there is a specific purpose to be fulfilled; a reason for which they were created.

To even approach this thought, we must understand that life is not the result of a cosmic accident. Rather, we must believe that God is the sovereign Creator and Sustainer of all things—animate and inanimate. If God is the creator and sustainer of our intricate and amazing universe, then logic tells us that He must be doing it all for a purpose, He must also have a divine plan for each of His creatures to fit into; a destiny which they were born to fulfill.

The Bible confirms this argument when it tells us that God knew us before our conception, and that He was involved in the gestational development of our physical form in our mothers' wombs (Jeremiah 1:5). It further tells us that God has plans for us, that His plans are for good and not evil, and we can have a perspective of hope because of His plans for us. (Jeremiah 29:11).

One of my greatest desires has been to help my children understand that God has created them for a purpose. It is an awesome responsibility to work with them to discover what the purpose is for their lives. I am not a psychologist, but I know in real terms that my children's self-concept—their understanding of who they are—and their positive feelings about themselves are directly linked to their understanding of the concept of a God-ordained purpose for their lives. Their ability to be content in life's circumstances comes from recognizing that to fulfill His plan, God has purpose and involvement in each situation they encounter.

I must be careful to see my children as God sees them and relate to them with the understanding that they have purpose defined from the heart of God. If I treat my children like they are an intrusion into my life—an unnecessary interruption in my schedule—rather than a precious gift from God, or if I act like they lack value or potential, instead of reinforcing to them their importance to God, or if I berate them and belittle them when they make a mistake rather than correct and instruct them in the proper methods and desired results, then my methods and my influence will not help them understand their unique purpose or lead them to achieve their destiny.

A father is to use his influence in their lives to help them discover their God-given destiny by developing and nurturing their strengths, desires, interests, and abilities.

The influence of a father is not to be used to predetermine or mold his children into what he wants them to be. Instead, he is to use his influence in their life to help them discover their God-given destiny by developing and nurturing their strengths, desires, interests, and abilities, and then encouraging them to go for it!

Discovering Purpose

I was in my early teens the first time I remember seriously considering what I was going to do with my life. I knew I wanted to marry and have a career like my dad. I wanted to be successful and influential like him. Pure and simple, I wanted to be like my dad!

When I graduated from college, I began to interview for employment. I talked to my dad's partners about working for their company. "You know, Tom," my dad kept reassuring me, "you do not have to do what I am doing."

My dad thoroughly enjoyed his work and his career, working for the same company for over 40 years. He started by filling orders in the warehouse, and he finished his career with the same company as a principal owner. He loved his work, but he also understood that although he loved it, I might not love it as he did. He did not want me to follow him into his business just to please him; he wanted me to find peace, happiness, and fulfillment as he had. These qualities are produced through knowing and fulfilling God's purpose.

As I have sought to guide my children in their search for purpose, I've kept two things in mind. First, I know that God designed each of my children for a unique purpose. God's plan for me may not be, and probably won't be, His plan for them. As their father, I am not to determine for them, or legislate on them, my predetermined idea for their life. My place rather, is to help them find God's unique purpose for their lives. Which brings me to my second thought: how can I help them do this? How can I best guide them without placing my own expectations and ambitions on them?

With these thoughts in mind, I have worked with my children to help them to discover and fulfill God's purpose for their life.

Guiding Children on the Road to Destiny

Many parents mistakenly think that they will send their son or daughter off to college when they are 18, and they'll "figure out" what they want to do with their lives through their college experience. Their college experience launches them into a career but not necessarily into their destiny, the groundwork for that must be laid before they get to college.

When Todd was months away from his fourteenth birthday. Jan and I learned about a summer mission program from a friend that was in town to minister at our church. He told us that his grandchildren had participated in it and that it had blessed and revolutionized their lives. As we discussed the mission organization and its thrust to provide teens with worldwide mission opportunities, my wife and I were impressed with the thought that this type of an experience might be good for Todd.

Jan and I have always tried to model for our children a commitment to serve God—*however*, *whenever*, and *wherever* that might take us.

We realized that Todd was entering the years when he would be making decisions that would determine his future, so we felt prompted to challenge him with a bigger view of the world. Todd was about to finish the eighth grade; he was looking with anticipation toward the move into high school that would come in the fall. But we were concerned that his high school experience would not encourage him to ask questions related to his purpose, or pose solutions that would be larger than the United States. We knew God was bigger than the United States. His Kingdom is all over the world, and the universe is His dwelling place. So we approached Todd with two options: he could go and work on one of 50 different summer mission projects with the worldwide mission organization our friend told us about, or he could attend a Christian high school in the fall. Unenthused about either option, he was particularly reluctant about the mission trip; it would mean giving up his whole summer before high school. Nevertheless, we wanted him to think globally for opportunities in his life and gain an experiential understanding and vision for life that was bigger than our town, state, or nation because the world is God's Kingdom, and consequently, God's work is worldwide. We wanted Todd to have this perspective as he considered his future and God's specific purpose for his life, so that he could consider the whole world as a possibility.

We had several discussions about his decision. The mission trip was expensive, costing about $2800. The mission organization strongly encouraged that the trip expense be raised through donations from family and friends, rather than paid by the parents. So, the three of us, Todd and Jan and I, arrived at this agreement: we would select a specific mission service project and submit the paperwork. In the meantime, we prayed that if it was *not* God's will for Todd to go he would *not* be accepted or the funds would *not* be contributed.

A few weeks later, Todd was accepted, and the support was raised from family and friends. God's will had been revealed and confirmed in his life. Todd spent the summer before high school in Ireland, building a recreation center at a Christian retreat facility. More significant than his work on the project though, is that he developed an awareness of God's work on a global scale.

Years later, when Todd graduated from college with a degree in finance, he went to work for an international corporation. His employment began in the United States but after a few years advancement opportunities took he and his wife to live in New Zealand. They lived in Auckland on assignment for his company, and became involved in a vibrant, growing church surrounded by many caring Christian friends. Their adjustment to a new country and culture, their success in finding a place of service, and their

To find God's purpose, you must be willing to obey and follow Him— wherever He may lead.

ability to build friendships were the result of the foundation developed through experiences like the summer mission project.

To find God's purpose, we must be willing to obey and follow Him—wherever He may lead. Business success is wonderful and brings with it financial rewards and freedom. But without an understanding of the higher purpose and call of God, the financial rewards and freedom they provide are tokens of an economic system but provide no eternal value or purpose. The things that last are those that we do out of an obedient heart for God and His Kingdom, things which fulfill God's divine plan for our lives. There is nothing more satisfying.

No Cookie Cutter Molds

As I have mentioned many times in this book Jan and I have four children. All of our children are now adults and three are married. Todd is our only child to have participated in a summer mission project. I say this to emphasize that the issue is not to send your children on a summer mission project, as good as that may be. The issue is to explore the uniqueness of God's plan for each child He entrusts to your care.

All four of our children are different. They are unique in personalities, abilities, talents, and interests. To find their destiny, they cannot be left to self-develop or be shoved into the same mold as each other or a mold I determine is best for them without consideration of God's plan for their life.

As parents, we must develop our children's desire to seek, find, and fulfill God's plan for their lives. Then, with guidance and oversight, we must allow our children to explore opportunities with the confidence that God will lead them to fulfill His purpose.

Parents often thwart their children's discovery of purpose because of legitimate concerns that are not handled properly. Discovery of purpose is a process in our children that can be confused with instability if not properly evaluated. Some parents have dreams for their children's future, living out their own unfulfilled desires through their lives. These parents do not support the discovery process unless it conforms to the dreams they have for their children. God intends to guide the children in their discovery of purpose and destiny through the parent-child relationship. Instead, a tug-of-war begins, the parents pushing their desires on the children and the children resisting, causing frustration and missed opportunities for both parties.

Three Steps to Destiny

What can you do to help your children discover and fulfill their destiny? Here are three guidelines to follow:

1. Teach your children that God is their Creator, and that He has a plan and a purpose for their life. Encourage your children in the discovery of their strengths, abilities, and interests. As you do this, your children will develop a proper perspective for the times when they fail—at a job, project, relationship, or commitment. Every person at some point fails; it is a part of life. Failing doesn't make them a failure; quitting does that.

You and I have learned from our mistakes; our children will learn from theirs. It is our role as parents to help them understand what went wrong and identify the characteristics that might be useful in understanding God's plan for their lives. We must do this without condemning or shaming them for not succeeding.

2. **Allow diversity to be a part of the discovery process.** I have a brother-in-law whose discovery of purpose developed through a different process than mine. However, he found a place of productivity and influence. In the early years of his adult life, he seemed unstable because he skipped from job to job in what seemed to be a whimsical approach to life. He seemed flighty and

> *...everyone who desires to serve and obey God will be directed by Him to fulfill His purpose.*

unfocused compared to the other men in our family. The other men and myself found our place more quickly without trying different jobs before discovering the purpose and direction God had for our lives.

Although it took my brother-in-law a little more time, he found and defined his purpose. The point is that not everyone will follow the same path to find God's plan and purpose for their life, but everyone who desires to serve and obey God will be directed by Him as they seek to discover and fulfill His purpose.

3. **Give priority attention to issues of character in your children.** Every parent must realize that there are tests to be passed on the road to fulfilling our destiny. To test the strength of our children's character, God determines and allows circumstances to come to pass in their lives. He will not move our children forward until they pass the grade level tests that He sends their way. God's

work in the process of their development will not excuse their character defects; therefore, we do our children no favors when we excuse them.

When you see laziness, slothfulness, disloyalty, rebellion, or other character flaws in your children, you must be diligent to address them. The younger your children are when you begin this process, the better. As your children grow into their upper teen years, the clay of their lives begins to harden, no longer being easily molded, until it becomes so hard that any change must be chiseled—sometimes pretty hard!—in order to bring conformity with God's purpose. Failure to give attention to issues of character is one reason that our children seem to get stuck in a repeating pattern of destructive failure. Their faulty character negatively influences their behavior and keeps them from discovering the fullness of God's purpose for their life.

A Concluding Thought

Francis of Assisi wrote:
> *"Keep a clear eye toward life's end. Do not forget your purpose and destiny as God's creature. What you are in His sight is what you are and nothing more..."*

How about you? Have you been aware of God's purpose and destiny for your life? Have you sought to raise your children with an understanding that God created them, and He has a plan for their lives? Have you seen something in the context of this chapter that you need to change in the way you relate to your children? If you will acknowledge your failure and ask for God's help, He will put your parenting influence back on the right track. *Why not do it right now?* As you turn to God today, He will give you wisdom and the ability to participate with your children in the discovery of their divine destiny!

CHAPTER 14
Raising Righteous Teens

The rod and rebuke give wisdom,
but a child left to himself
brings shame to his mother.

Proverbs 29:15

I spent most of my teen years looking ahead to the next season of my life and resenting people who looked down on my age. I felt I was mature and capable of handling more responsibility than most adults gave me credit. Talk to almost any teenager and you will find some version of these feelings being played out in his life. By definition, a teenager is a person between the ages of thirteen and nineteen years. The teenage years are an awkward stage of development between childhood and adulthood that present some very interesting challenges to the parenting process. When relating to a teenager, sometimes you don't know which person to relate to — the child we know, or the adult beginning to emerge.

Consider the paradoxes represented in these statements about teenagers and see if you can see your teen in them. A teenager is a person who can't remember to take out the trash but never forgets a phone number. A teenager diets by giving up candy bars before breakfast. A teenager is someone who can hear a song by Madonna played three blocks away but can't hear his mother calling from the next room. A teenager can operate the latest computer, video game, or electronic gadget without a lesson but can't remember to make his bed or take out the trash. He has the time and energy to play GAME BOY for hours, or talk on the phone past midnight, but doesn't have strength to help with chores around the house. A teenager struggles to make it to dinner, work, or class on time but isn't a minute late for a rock concert or a date. A teenager is a person who believes his thoughts are original and innovative yet is convinced his parents were never younger than thirty!

The teenage years are important and bring unique challenges and opportunities as does each stage of development. Parents of young children are in complete control directing every aspect of their child's life to impart values and to encourage proper actions. As children grow toward adulthood, parenting becomes less about directing and more about advising. A parent ultimately occupies the role of advisor or mentor in his adult child's life.

Both of our parents have served in that capacity in our lives. Although they respect us as adults, they have served as influential advisors on major decisions impacting our life and our future.

During each of your child's developmental stages, your responsibility is to guide him along the path of life, imparting values, developing and defining talents, and creating a self-concept based on a present awareness of God and His love. In the years leading to adulthood, the process of parenting enters a new and critical stage. The teenage years are the final stage of self-discovery that determines whether your son or daughter becomes an adult prepared to fulfill God's purpose independent from your direct control but not apart from your guiding influence.

3 THINGS EVERY TEEN NEEDS

There are three things your teen needs more than ever during this stage of his or her life.

First, your teen needs to know how much you care about _him_. Communicating to him that you understand the demands and pressures he faces is critical for success. Knowing you care is not enough. This knowledge must be linked with understanding to his feelings. When this happens it communicates empathy for what they are experiencing and establishes a bond with your teenager.

Second, he needs to know the "why" and the "how" of what you believe. Often they need to debate it and test it to know exactly how it worked for you and to see how to make it work for his life. Forcing your teen to adopt your values through a legalistic enforcement of what you want will guarantee rebellion. The best course of action is to ask your teen to accept your values and explain your reason for adopting the values in your own life. You must show him how your values have worked for you and help him to apply them to his life. If you embark on a shared process with your teen that helps him form and discover his values for living then you will establish yourself as his partner for life.

The third thing every teen needs is clearly defined boundaries and accountability in the context of a loving relationship. This is the most common area where parents fall short in relating to their teens. Finding a balance in this area is difficult but failure to do so results in one of two extremes. One end of the extreme sets both the boundaries and accountability too tight, which causes the teen to chafe under the "mean rules" and ultimately to rebel. The other end of the extreme makes the boundaries so loose as to be non-existent, causing the teen to self-develop. In order to help your teen find and develop his values, you do not have to become a drill sergeant nor do you have to become so removed that he is on his own. In fact, the best way to establish boundaries and enforce accountability is around mutually agreed upon values. This takes work and, more importantly, it takes a relationship with your teenager!

5 CONCEPTS NECESSARY FOR SUCCESSFUL ADULT LIVING

By now I hope you understand the principle of transference. It is the underlying theme of this book. The principle of transference is the idea that your children will adopt and embrace the values and qualities actively demonstrated from your life. You've heard the statement, "I am sorry, I can't hear what you are saying, your actions are speaking too loudly." This is the mantra of the teenage generation. It is a reminder that your values must be modeled for your children if you want them to transfer. I just want to say again that your actions are a much more influential tutor than the instruction of your words or the concepts you believe but do not practice! As I share these five concepts, it is important that you live them. If you do not, they will ring hollow with your teen.

1. <u>We need a comprehension of God, His love, His ways, and His involvement in our life</u>. In the book of Matthew, chapter 22, a religious leader asked Jesus, "Teacher, which is the greatest commandment in the law?" Jesus' answer was simple yet profound: "You shall love the Lord your God with all your heart, with all your soul, and with all your mind". In other words, our love for God should permeate every aspect of our life. No situation is outside of God's loving care and involvement. No situation at work, school, with teachers or others in authority, with friends or family is outside

of God's involvement and care.

It was this perspective that led to a conversation with Tyler during his junior year of high school. I noticed that his attitude had become careless about authority. He was critical of teachers and the school administration. He was grumpy about work and the people he worked with and I noticed that he was driving too fast. I talked to him about this carelessness but he ignored it. After a few days with no noticed change, I brought it up again and reminded him that God was interested in his attitude toward authority. He took a little more notice but not much. Then one Friday evening as I was coming home from work, I noticed the strobe of police lights ahead as I drove toward my home. An officer had pulled two cars over along the street leading to our house. As I pulled down the street I recognized one of the cars as Tyler's. I pulled behind the police officer and walked to the driver's window of Tyler's car. As I approached, I could see Tyler slide down in the seat. I greeted him with a "What's up Tyler" just as the officer returned with the ticket for drag racing. The officer greeted me with, "You must be the dad?" I said, "Yes I am and I appreciate the fine job you are doing. Is there anything you need me to do?" He said, "No things are handled here." I turned to Tyler and said, "I will see you at home."

This incident was an object lesson in God's interest in the little details of Tyler's life. His careless attitude was noticed by me but ignored by him. God cared enough to insert a different authority to deal with his attitude before something more serious happened. God has ways to discipline us for our responses. This time it was a ticket, a court appearance and a fine. My view of life tells me this is not just bad luck, or the way life is, but it is God inserting Himself into the circumstances of life to deal with us because He loves us!

During their teen years my children came to understand God's loving care and involvement in their lives. I transferred this concept to them through numerous situations like the one above where I reminded them of God's interest and involvement in their lives. It was our parenting that gave them this perspective as they developed.

2. <u>We must see a God-centered purpose for our life</u>.

As a Christian, I see life as having purpose ordered by God. I see it in a macro sense in nature and world events and I see it in a micro sense related to my life. God created me (and you) with a purpose in mind. Discovering our purpose is one of the most important quests of life. Jeremiah 29:11 tells us about God's view of us—- that God knows us and thinks about us every moment. He has plans for good and peace, plans with a future and a hope and not plans of evil toward us. The most important thing any of us can do is ask and answer the question, "What does God want me to do?"

In the last chapter I gave an account of how we helped transfer this concept to our oldest son, Todd. Beyond our influence we wanted his destiny in God to be reinforced in a tangible way so we talked with him about spending the summer before high school on a mission trip. We worked with him to help him discover how God could lead and provide for something like this if it is His desire and plan for his development. To him, it was a waste of his summer— an understandable teenage perspective. Through varied experiences and our guidance, our children learned to live their lives with God's plan in mind.

Each of our four children has embraced the concept that God created them in their mother's womb and He has a plan for their lives. Although the concept of a God-centered purpose for life has been transferred to each of our children, they grasped the concept in different ways unique to their own life.

3. <u>We must understand the importance of a good name</u>.

Sometimes it seems unfair but the truth is, we are known by the company we keep. Our reputation is influenced by the circle of our friends. We must guard against an attitude of pride or superiority that would lead us to think of ourselves as better than other people. The importance of a good name is not about race, economic standing, or social status. It is about values. Proverbs Chapter 22 says it this way, "A good name is to be chosen rather than great riches, loving favor rather than silver and gold." A good name is the reason we keep our word and have as our close friends those who also value keeping their word. Although we are friendly to all people, we do not make close friendships with people of bad reputation unless they are willing to change their ways and be influenced by our values.

Simply stated the concept is this: peer pressure is a powerful thing. Used properly, it makes us better. If peer pressure is ignored or taken lightly it will result in our children being influenced to do wrong things by their friends. The influence of bad friends can not be over estimated. The effect over time is what leads them to make bad life choices and ultimately what influences them to call what is good bad and what is bad good. The apostle Paul wrote to the Corinthian church that bad company corrupts good habits! This truth is not age-specific but is important to be learned and embraced early in life. To do so will save a lot of heartache throughout life. We must monitor who our children hang out with and the impact of friends on their behavior and their attitudes.

4. <u>We must understand that character, diligence, and faithfulness are developed through adversity</u>.

In our community each fall there is a county fair. We used to tell our kids when they came home complaining about the unfairness of something that there is only one fair and it is in the fall! I realize that one of the responsibilities of a parent is to be the protector and defender of his children. I am not saying that we abandon that responsibility. I am saying that a companion responsibility to protecting our children is building strength of character in them. Strength of character is the ability to do what is right when someone is looking AND when no one is looking. Diligence is the capacity to keep doing something when the rewards are slow in coming. Faithfulness is the quality of accepting and acting with responsibility and loyalty in all the affairs of life.

The enemy to developing these qualities in our teens is a three-headed monster. First, it is the hurts from our past that cause us to make vows that begin with "I will never" or end with "I will always", so that when some injustice touches our children we can't help them deal with it through trust in God and forgiveness.

Instead, we become offended for them and act based on the vow made previously because of a hurt or experience in our own life.

Second, it is attitudes of enabling that shield our children from every possible adversity of life. When our children come whimpering to us, we enable their inability to deal with life by acting on their behalf. The result is that we teach them there are no consequences to their behavior, leading them to believe that life will always be fair and if it is not, someone (other than God) will make it right for them. How does this fit with Jesus' statement in John chapter 16 that the world will cause us tribulation? The comfort that Jesus gave was the fact that He had overcome the world. Jesus is the answer to every injustice.

Finally, it is failed expectations that we place on others which adversely touch our children. It might be that we expect a friend who is coaching to draft our child or that we expect a business associate to hire our child or show favor. Unfulfilled expectations create disappointment that leads to hurt and offense which in turn, gets in the way of our ability to help our children see God's hand in the circumstances that have disappointed them.

5. We must understand the importance of relational and social skills.

The Bible indicates that God's plan for humanity incorporates all His work into relationships. It was because of God's love for us that Jesus came to redeem lost and fallen man. We reflect God's nature when we relate to each other with love and kindness. Teaching this concept begins by showing our children how to respond with honor and respect to adults and continues as we teach them how to play with friends. It doesn't stop there but carries through each stage of development on their way to their teen years, where they learn to respond in dating relationships. The dynamics of human relationship make it the most complicated relationship known to man. In order to relate in healthy ways we must teach our children how to communicate, how to confront, how to resolve conflict, how to express affection, and how to be loyal and committed to family and friends.

A Concluding Thought

Parenting is not an exact science; it is a process. No parent is perfect because no human is perfect. When our children leave home to assume responsibility for their lives, we can guarantee a successful adjustment if we give them the tools. The concepts covered in this chapter are the tools they need to succeed as adults. It is never too late to begin the process. Regardless of the ages of your children or their development stage, begin today to be an influential parent to them. Help your children progress into adulthood by teaching them to apply these important concepts to their lives.

CHAPTER 15

Helping Teens Handle Social Pressure

Do not be deceived: Evil company corrupts good habits.

1 Corinthians 15:33

God has created each of us with appetites that yearn to be satisfied. Appetites are intended to drive us toward life sustaining resources necessary for health and life. Some of these appetites we are familiar with but some we may not have identified although we have lived with them our whole life.

The five areas of appetite are for: food, sex, pleasure, status, and God (or spiritual life). Since God created these appetites, He also created the means by which these appetites can be satisfied in a healthy and beneficial way. For your teenager to be prepared for the temptations, opportunities and challenges of adulthood he must learn how to manage these appetites in an emotionally, physically, and spiritually healthy way.

From the time our children first interact with friends, they are thrust into situations that pressure them to respond to their developing appetites, often in ways that are unhealthy. The question facing them at each stage of development is the same one that faces us as adults in pressured situations: "Who or what will influence the decisions of my life? How will we satisfy the cravings of our appetites?

Will the appetite that is craving fulfillment be satisfied by the quickest fix available? Will the appetite for pleasure be influenced by friends or be satisfied as God intended? Will the appetite for status or the appetite for sex be satisfied according to the accepted morals of our culture or will these appetites be satisfied as God desires; through humility and hard work; within the context of a committed marriage relationship?

Monitoring the Influences of Friends

When our children first began playing with friends, we monitored the effect of their play. We monitored both their actions and their attitudes. After playing with a friend, if we found that our child's attitude was rebellious or disrespectful or his behavior was such that he knew we would not approve, we restricted or eliminated his play with that friend. It is our responsibility as parents to teach our children how to live the Biblical values we impart even in the face of pressure to act otherwise. At every stage of development, we must teach our children the best way to handle the pressure to act against our values, teaching them to fulfill appetites in healthy ways. If we fail to do this at the age of four, five and six, we have forfeited our prime opportunity to train these appetites. God never intended for us to begin training our children in their teen years to manage their appetites.

Jan and I have been diligent to do this training with each of our children. The situations were different with each child but the method was the same. It was not our desire to dominate their life but to make sure that the good habits we were seeking to develop in them were not corrupted or undone by the influence of friends or people who did not hold our same values. We could not let the worldly influences around them teach them how to satisfy their appetites. We had to be proactive in parenting our teenagers. Sometimes, the issue wasn't that our children's friends had different values — their families had the same values as ours. The issue was that our children and certain ones of their friends did not influence each other in good ways as they played together. So we had to take action for their mutual benefit. Such was the case with one of Tyler's friends. Michael was the son of a couple who were friends of ours. He was a sweet, fun-loving boy who was pleasant to be around. Tyler and Michael played together from the time they were born; they were best friends. As they got older, they were both active boys to the point that my friend Jimmy Evans dubbed them the "hyper-twins".

About the time the "hyper-twins" turned eight years old, we began to notice that they got into mischief when they played together. For instance, one day the boys were left alone to play together while Michael's mom ran a short errand. They were playing in Michael's garage and found some cans of spray paint. In a playful moment, one of the boys removed the cap from one of the cans and sprayed it into the air. No harm done, so the other boy did the same. That playful moment led to one boy spray-painting a swoosh on the wall which, in turn, led to the other boy copying with another swoosh. They spent the next hour or so spray-painting the garage walls with their eight-year-old version of graffiti art. You can imagine the response of Michael's mom when she arrived home to find the boys' handy work. Both of these boys knew better than to spray the garage wall with paint but neither could stop the other from doing what they both knew to be wrong. Their appetites for pleasure and status were being fulfilled through unhealthy behavior and neither boy was influencing the other to do what they knew was right.

This was not a singular, isolated event but a growing trend that led us to decide that the boys could not play together. We told them they would not be able to play together again until they could influence each other's behavior in a positive way. I don't remember exactly how long it was before they were allowed to play together again but I do remember that it was months, not just a few days.

A detailed explanation about their appetites was not a part of our teaching; only how to manage them. As parents, we knew their appetites were governing their behavior. We also knew that we had to teach our children to satisfy their appetites properly to get the behavior we knew was right. When they resumed play, they did so with an awareness of their responsibility to be a good influence on each other. They have remained good friends even to this day. Last year, Michael was a groomsman in Tyler's wedding.

Addressing Temptations

Teens are presented with a variety of temptations as they grow up. Temptations are nothing more than an opportunity to satisfy an appetite— usually in an unhealthy way. We cannot ignore these temptations or assume that because our kids have the influence of church in their lives, or because they have been raised in our home to know our values, that they will be able to resist either the temptations or the peer pressures that pull at them on a daily basis. We must teach them how to satisfy their appetites in a Godly, biblical and healthy way.

Proactive parenting must take a position on drugs, premarital sex, drinking, attitudes toward authority, and a whole host of other issues affecting life. We must not only take a position, but also communicate our position regularly to our children while we monitor their acceptance of our standards and their ability to stand firm in the face of temptation and pressure.

We can't assume that other parents hold our same values or that they will be as vigilant in monitoring or enforcing them as we are with our children. One of the steps we took as our children entered their teens was to enforce a "party policy". When one of our children came home and told us that he or she had been invited to a party at a friend's house, we asked to see the invitation. Without exception, we saw rolled eyes and a response as if we were from Mars. We were the old, out-of-touch people, unaware that kids do not send out formal invitations to parties— their invitations are by word-of-mouth. Although that is the kids' accepted method of extending an invitation, our children could not attend one of these parties unless we had one of these things: either a formal invitation or a conversation with the parent of the teen having the party to make sure they were aware of the party and to confirm they were going to be home chaperoning what was taking place. The goal here was not to prevent our children from attending parties but to help them avoid situations that were too pressure-filled for them to handle and to teach them how to have fun in a healthy way. We consistently applied this policy and, after a few times, the kids knew without exception what was needed to get our okay. The parties they did attend were properly chaperoned where teens were having fun without breaking the law or hurting themselves.

In Chapter Four, I referred to my position on drinking as I related a story that involved my oldest son and a souvenir beer bottle he brought home. I thought it better to give a more complete explanation in this chapter about my position rather than explain myself in the context of the story. Substance abuse in many forms is something that our children will be exposed to and they must have an answer. They don't need to experiment on their own to find the answer— it is our parental responsibility to help them. That is why it is important for us to help them understand their appetites and to work with them to find God's method of satisfying them.

First, let me say I believe in having fun. I enjoy life to its fullest and I want my children to do the same. However, I do not hold to the belief that part of growing up is to go through a phase of "sowing your wild oats" in order to find yourself. I don't think you have to experience something to avoid it. For instance, I have never been in jail and I have no desire to be in jail. I haven't had to experience jail to form that opinion. Parental attitudes regarding substance abuse vary based on personal experience and personal use. There are a variety of things which are abused and are illegal to be consumed by teenagers, such as drugs, alcohol, glue, and cigarettes. While not exhaustive, this list does represent things that, as parents, we want our children to learn about and handle in a healthy and responsible way. Parental involvement is not only necessary, it is essential in guiding our children to healthy and responsible behavior. We must teach them how to satisfy their appetites for pleasure and status among their friends.

Once again let me say that to transfer a value to our children we must "walk the walk" before we "talk the talk". This is true related to how we handle substances. Have you learned to satisfy your appetites in a healthy way? Do you model that for your children to see? How can we guide our children related to substances if we abuse them ourselves?

My response to drinking alcohol is based on an overall response to substance abuse and is based on an understanding of how to satisfy an appetite for pleasure and status in a way sanctioned by God. It is not based on religious feelings of performance or emotions of guilt; it is based on my value system. Although my values are founded on the principles of the Bible, they were impacted and shaped by personal experience as well.

My first exposure to drinking came when I was in junior high school. In Sunday school each week, the high school boys would tell wild stories of their drinking and drunken escapades from Friday and Saturday nights. It always struck me as inconsistent that they would be carrying their Bibles and talking about God in the same context as their drinking escapades. Hypocrisy is a religious coat that Jesus opposed wherever he encountered it because it replaces a personal relationship with God with a false front. We certainly don't want to wear that coat nor pass it on for our children to wear.

I was raised in a home where drinking was accepted. When I began high school, my dad sat me down and told me that I would be exposed to alcohol. He asked me to come to him if I was ever interested in trying it, and he would give me what I wanted from his supply at home. He told me he would rather do that than have me experiment on my own and drive under the influence of alcohol. I never took my dad up on his offer, but during my high school years, I knew the offer was on the table. It may have been part of the reason I never became interested. I knew I did not have to try alcohol in secret to find out what it was all about.

One other experience had influence on the way I viewed alcohol. The dad of one of my close high school friends was an alcoholic. I saw firsthand the pain that my friend experienced when his dad would disappear on a multi-day drinking binge. I never went with him when he went to find his dad and bring him home, but I imagined how awful that would be and decided I wanted nothing to do with something so destructive. There had to be a different way to satisfy an appetite for pleasure.

As I have been exposed to different cultures around the world and have grown in my knowledge of the Bible, my experiences have joined with what I now know are the Bible's parameters on this subject. More important than my experiences are the Bible's instruction related to these appetites and the healthy way to satisfy them.

When I sat down to instruct my children, I shared with them the experiences outlined above. I told them that I had chosen not to drink alcohol in order to have the greatest influence on people, and to eliminate any risk of its damaging effect on my life and the lives of people influenced by me.

Alcohol and drugs, in my view, are risks. When people drink or take drugs, they risk addiction, they risk their reputations, they risk their employment or their businesses; they put at risk everything important in life. Life is filled with risks. Many of these risks are out of our control. Therefore, we have to depend on God to protect us from the risks that are beyond our control. But I see the risk related to drugs and alcohol as something I can control by the choices I make and the lifestyle I live.

In teaching my children about their appetites and the temptations to satisfy them, I shared the Bible's perspective along with my experiences. As I taught my children I understood that my perspective is my own—I knew that they would have to make their own decisions related to the values they held for their life. I understood that ultimately their decision would be between them and God.

It was my desire that they would agree with my values and adopt them as their own, but I could not make them do so. I shared my perspective to give them guidance, but each one had to come to a decision for his or her own life on the way each would find pleasure, satisfaction and purpose. However, as they made their decisions, I wanted each to talk with me about what had been decided so that I would know what to expect and so that I could keep each accountable for his or her decision.

As a part of forming their decisions, I gave them what I believed was the Biblical perspective on satisfying their appetites in a healthy manner so they could factor that into their choices. Regardless of their decisions, whether they were the same as mine or not, they knew they would have to live within Biblical boundaries to experience God's blessing in their lives. Here are the Biblical guidelines I gave them:

1. Be submitted to the governing authorities and their laws. That means no teenage drinking (Romans 13:1). Underage drinking and illicit drug use are against the laws of the United States.

2. Consider the influence your action might have on others before you act, even if it is within biblical boundaries. Paul gave a charge in his letter to the Romans that Christians are not to live to themselves (Romans 14:7). It is my experience that when a person wants his life to be an example of his love for Christ, the good intention loses its influence when associated with self-gratification and personal indulgences. Even though you may have freedom to indulge within proper boundaries (for instance, to drink if you are of legal

age, and not drink to excess) someone may observe your example and use it to justify their wrong behavior. Or another person may observe your behavior and be offended. In his first letter to the Corinthians, Paul encouraged them to be sensitive to matters of conscience in the people around them. Since it is difficult to know who is watching and how they might perceive your behavior even if it is within legal or Biblical parameters, I choose not to drink (I Corinthians 8:9-13).

3. Your reputation is important for God's further use and placement of you in responsible positions of authority in His Kingdom. Consider the impact of your behavior on your reputation. The qualifications for church leadership raise a high standard related to many areas of life and personal conduct. For instance, the Bible states that an elder must not be given to wine (I Timothy 3:3). I told my children that if they aspire to leadership in God's Kingdom and in His church, they must sacrifice their personal liberties and must conduct themselves in a manner that reflects God's nature and character.

4. Appearance of wrong can create as many problems as a wrong act itself. So it is important to consider how and where your fun takes place. When the Bible presents drinking in an acceptable light, it is related to celebration. Practically speaking, when our adult children become of legal age to drink we did not forbid them to drink because the Bible does not forbid drinking. It does say that the alcohol-related celebrating cannot be immoral, involve drunkenness, or include carousing (Galatians 5:19).

5. Experimenting with pleasure or hedonistic self-gratification is dangerous. If we seek God we will find pleasure in Him. The Greek word for sorcery is "pharmica" which we translate into pharmacy. No where in the Bible is illicit drug use condoned in any form; in fact a case can be made that it

is associated with idol worship. While we use drugs for medical purposes we do not experiment with them and they are never to control us. They are not to be abused for self-gratification or pleasure.

I have told my children that should they choose not to embrace my perspective as their own, I would be disappointed but I will always love them. The choice was theirs and I would respect their choice. However, regardless of their choice I taught them that they were not free to live outside of the Biblical parameters listed above. All of our children have embraced the values Jan and I have taught and modeled as their own.

A Concluding Thought

It was not my purpose in this chapter to present my perspective as something that you have to embrace. My purpose is to remind you that as parents, we must give our children guidance in how to conduct their lives and satisfy their God-given appetites. We must challenge our children through our own behavior, and the values we transfer to them, to live a life of influence for God.

What I would say to all parents is this: you must define, communicate, and model your values clearly for your children to understand and embrace them as their own. Your children need guidance as they form their moral and spiritual values for living. To help them, you must have searched the Scriptures and defined God's perspective on the issues. You also must be proactive with your children regarding the pressures and temptations they face and provide guidance as they form their responses.

Successful parenting of teenagers involves teaching them to fulfill their immerging and raging appetites in Godly and healthy ways. Have you learned to do that in your own life? Are you proactively involved with your teens? They need your active involvement and instruction as they finish their preparation for adulthood. It's not too late to begin influencing them to satisfy their appetites in Godly and healthy ways even if your children are grown. Your influence as a parent and grandparent has long lasting generational effect, you can act now to be the influence God desires.

CHAPTER 16

Remember The Big Picture: It Ain't Over 'Til It's Over

What are we as parents to do when our troubled young adults return home? Receive them with open arms? We raised them once, is it our responsibility to do it a second and third time?

When Jan and I began our family, I assumed that my parental responsibilities would be over once my children reached adult age. I was mistaken. Over the years, I've found the statement "once a parent always a parent" to be true. Although parenting responsibilities change as children get older, they never completely disappear.

Both the Bible and archaeological discovery from past civilizations provide models that confirm the premise of lifetime parenting. Before the advent of planes, trains, and automobiles, when mobility was limited, people naturally assumed that their families would grow together. In Jesus' day, people were born, married, and buried all within a few hundred square miles. Travel was not only slow by today's standards—it was dangerous. Families stayed together, affording each new generation the influence and example of the previous generation.

Today's society offers more choices, often to the peril of the family unit. Children grow up and leave home to pursue education, start careers, and raise families, often moving hundreds of miles away from brothers, sisters, parents, grandparents, aunts, uncles, and cousins. The diminished family influence allows pressures and influences to come to children that do not come as easily when there is family connection. Without the network of family support, wrong influences pressure them with greater success, turning them away from the values that their parents have worked hard to instill in them. As they search for identity and purpose, they are left alone to respond to destructive influences, competing for their lives and forced to ride out turbulent waves of pressured influence on their own.

The last two generations have particularly suffered in this way. As mobility has increased, families have fractured. More than half of all marriages fail today. Children are left out in the cold, lacking the nurturing influence of the family. Even those who are nurtured are often pulled from the stability and strength of family and extended family, by the mobility of our society as they roam further and further to pursue pleasure, education, and careers. When our children hit turbulent waters and their lives are turned upside down by divorce, job loss, drug abuse, or any number of factors, they often find themselves without the support and accountability of their families. Increasingly, we see young adults in crisis—victims of a mobile society with changing values and shifting morality—returning home to the place of their roots for support and regrouping.

What are we as parents to do when our troubled young adults return home? Receive them with open arms? We raised them once. Is it our responsibility to do it a second and third time?

RESPONDING TO WRONG BEHAVIOR

Knowing how to respond to children who are in crisis is especially difficult when the situation is a result of wrong choices that they have made. Instinct tells us that it might be best for our children to pay for their mistakes, especially when they have either not sought our input or they have flat out rejected it as they created their mess. In these situations, we may feel justified to be critical, or we may feel it necessary to invoke tough love because we have been rejected and are disappointed as we watch them make choices that do not reflect the values we have imparted to them over the years. So a response that lets them know, *"you got yourself into this mess; you can get yourself out of it,"* seems the right solution. But is it? "How else will they learn their lessons?" you ask.

Our loving intention is to drive home a point. We want them to wake up and *learn from their mistakes.* We want to make sure our children do not repeat their blunder, so we attempt to control them, to fix their wrong behavior, and we often do it with a condescending, "I told you so" attitude. This response will not change our children's behavior; instead, it erects barriers that keep them removed from our love and the influence they need.

What is the correct way to respond? What is a parent to do? Knowing how to respond requires wisdom. What seems natural by instinct oftentimes does not reflect God's nature; it just vents our frustration. The way we respond cannot enable our children's wrong

You must allow them freedom of choice, and be willing to forgive and restore relationship when there is a right response, not holding their mistakes over their heads indefinitely.

behavior, but neither should it completely reject them, leaving them no avenue for return. Looking to God as our model for response, here is what we must do: we must be gracious and kind, yet not compromise the standard of our beliefs. We must allow them freedom of choice, and be willing to forgive and restore relationship when there is a right response, not holding their mistakes over their heads indefinitely. Of course, it is easier said than done.

Dwayne came to my office broken hearted by choices that his son was making, and he was at a loss to know how he should respond. His son, Kelly, had filed for divorce after 6 years of marriage. Dwayne knew that Kelly and Carrie were struggling; he had observed increased tension between them. But he struggled to support the decision Kelly made to leave the marriage that also included two children.

Dwayne tried to talk his son into taking another route to solve his problem but he could not move his thinking from his decision to divorce his wife. In addition to filing for divorce, he quit a stable, good paying job and planned to pursue a dream of owning his own business. Kelly's hobby was motorcycles. He told has dad that he intended to buy a motorcycle shop and race motorcycles. Kelly did not care who didn't like it; his mind was made up.

Dwayne came to me to discuss what he should do to help Kelly. This is the dilemma many parents find themselves in with their adult children. As parents should we attempt to force them to do what we think is best? If we disagree with their decisions do we continue a relationship with them, never making their decision an issue between us?

Each situation requires God's wisdom. There is great emotional trauma in these circumstances for all involved. Especially when one parent wants to exercise tough love and the other wants to extend open arms to the child regardless of their mistakes. My counsel to Dwayne was to follow the path of the prodigal father. I encouraged him not to attempt to control or manipulate his son. I acknowledged how hard it would be for Dwayne and his wife, to release their son to make decisions that would bring hurt now and possible regret later. In addition, I advised him not to cut off relationship with Kelly, but also not to compromise what he felt was right in order to maintain the relationship.

I reminded Dwayne that God allows each of us to make our own choice, to follow Him or to go our own way, even though He knows the full and final destruction associated with our decision. He stands ready to receive us if or when we return to Him broken by the results of our decision. Prayer is the appropriate place for us to pour out our concern, frustration, and passionate plea for action. God is the only one who knows all things and can arrange circumstances to apply the right pressure to jog our children's thinking in a way that does not violate their freedom of choice but does a work to change their heart returning them to what they know is right.

FATHERS BUILD BRIDGES FOR THEIR CHILDREN

The story of the prodigal son is found in Luke 15. It is a story of a young son who rejects his father's advice, makes a series of wrong choices, only to return home after making a mess of his life. This biblical story could have been drawn from many family situations in America today. It is as current as this morning's news.

The parable Jesus told is a picture of how God the Father responds to His children. The account provides two key revelations for parents. First, it reveals the way to respond to actions of independence and what seems to be wayward behavior in our adult children. Second, it provides parents a model to follow, showing them the way to relate to their adult children by treating the relationship in such a way that will build and maintain the bridge for their child's return back to the values imparted to them while they were in our home. Proverbs tells us that if we raise a child in the way he should go when he is old he won't depart from the training. He may divert but he won't depart! That is a promise to hold on to!

The story goes like this: The younger of two sons approaches his father and asks for an early distribution of the inheritance coming to him. The son's request carries with it a rejection of the family and implies a loathing attitude for the family business. He wants to head out on his own.

The father apportions his possessions, giving the youngest son what is rightfully his. The son promptly leaves home, and through a series of bad decisions, wastes his inheritance on riotous or prodigal living. Whatever prodigal living might have been, it is safe to say the son was living and making choices that were not

> *A father's primary responsibility is to reveal God to his children by teaching them about Him and His ways.*

consistent with the values his father had imparted to him. After some time, the wayward son spent all his inheritance and made a mess of his life, a path not unlike the ones some young people take on their journey to adulthood.

The waves of life had shipwrecked the young son, and he found himself in a desperate situation. The story says:

> *"...when he came to himself, he said, '...I will arise and go to my father...' "* (Luke 15:17-18)

In other words, the son took inventory of his life and the mess he had created and realized it was not what he wanted, so he decided to go home. He hoped that his father would take him back as a servant and provide him with room and board in exchange for work.

His father was not obligated to help his son according to custom, since he had disassociated himself from the family by taking his inheritance and departing. In fact, his father was entitled to treat him as dead, to respond as though he never existed. The prodigal son would have been aware of his father's right, yet he reasoned that if his father would take him back—not as a son, but as a lowly servant—it would be better than the situation he had made for himself.

What is the responsibility of a father to his children? When has the responsibility been fulfilled? The answer to that question forms the foundation for the response the father made to his prodigal son. It is the answer we need to embrace as we respond to the wayward behavior of our children.

A father's primary responsibility is to reveal God to his children by teaching them about God and His ways. He is responsible to help his children find eternal purpose for their lives. The fulfillment of this responsibility takes consistent input and guidance throughout their life. All children search for identity and purpose. Some break away from the guidance of their parents as they search. A wise father will build and maintain the bridge necessary for his children to come home.

WHEN CHILDREN RETURN HOME

In the story, the father not only took his wayward son back, but also restored his rights as a son, receiving him with celebration. This response is uncharacteristic of many fathers who have had children go their own ways, especially when the children's choices have ended in disaster. The father's response serves as a pattern to be followed by all fathers, because it is a representation of God's response to each of us. Notice that the father's response to his wayward son accomplished four things:

1. It recognized his son's need to find significance.

2. It allowed his son a process of discovery in his search.
3. It acknowledged his son's ability to make choices, but refused to enable his wrong behavior.
4. It kept the focus on the completed search and the enduring fruit it would produce.

Discovering the purpose for which we were created is the only way to fully satisfy the search for personal significance in our lives.

When we learn to incorporate this four-fold pattern of response, we will further God's work in our children's lives and help them discover their purpose, even if their search takes a rocky road. Let's look more closely at the father's responses and what they accomplished.

THE SEARCH FOR SIGNIFICANCE

The search for significance is common to all humanity. It is the homing mechanism in the heart of man that is designed to motivate him to search for God. Discovering the purpose for which we were created is the only way to fully satisfy the search for personal significance in our lives. Our fullest and deepest purpose can only be found through relationship with God. The process of discovery has many roads; we do not all arrive by the same one. Regardless of the road taken, everyone hungers to know his or her purpose.

It is critical for parents to understand that God has built the desire to know our purpose into the human fabric. Personal contentment and happiness are directly linked to the purpose for which we were created. Therefore, helping our children discover their significance is critical. God created children unique in personalities, physical attributes, and abilities, and He has a specific plan for their lives.

As our children search for significance, we must understand that the discovery process is not always smooth or convenient, or the method of our choosing. We must also remember that our children's self-esteem is closely connected to the discovery process. Just like us, our children seek to satisfy their needs for identity, purpose, acceptance, and security. Their search begins by identifying mechanisms that supply these basic needs, and the fulfillment of the needs provides a foundation for significance. The standards and training we model and transfer to our children help them know the good and acceptable ways to satisfy their needs.

> *The first work of God in your life is to guide you to discover your uniqueness in Him.*

In the parable, the father released his son, without apparent resistance, to search for his own significance. Our sons and daughters will not find their significance in the fulfillment of plans, goals, and desires we have determined best for their lives, regardless of how noble they seem. They must identify their plans, goals, and desires for themselves; our role is to provide encouragement and guidance for them in the process of their search.

Several years ago, we had a young, single woman come live with us. She was a wonderful blessing to our family. She had completed college and was working as a nurse.

One evening as we were talking about her frustration with work, the discussion turned to her choice of nursing as a career. To my surprise, I found that she hated nursing; she only did it because it was her degree field. So I asked her, "If you hate nursing, why did you choose it?" She told me it was not her choice; her parents picked it for her. They told her nursing would provide her with a career that would enable her to support herself and not depend on anyone else.

I understand the care and concern behind this parental logic; however, there was one fatal flaw: they did not allow their daughter to discover and hold this purpose as her own. They determined what was best for her without considering what was in her heart. This young woman was out of college, in a career she hated, living away from her parents, and supporting herself; but she was nowhere close to finding and understanding her personal significance. How could she know or find her significance when her parents had never validated her identity as unique before God?

The first work of God in our lives is to guide us to discover our uniqueness in Him. Therefore, our first responsibility as parents is to help our children find their significance. One way we do this is by communicating to them that they have a unique identity created by God in their mother's womb.

During the children's developmental years, we must help them define their purpose and guide them in their search for significance. As they mature into adults, we can pray for them, encourage them, and support their search for the most important ingredient in human personal satisfaction—the knowledge of their created purpose. The process requires that we recognize their right to choose a road we would not choose for them if that is their desire. Even though we anticipate the pain their choice will potentially cause them, we cannot force them to do what we believe best because it violates their God given right to choose. God does not force us to choose His way, even though He knows the benefit of such a decision. He allows us to make the choice not to follow His will, to His grief, and to our eternal detriment.

People who feel significant have discovered three important factors. First, they have made a connection between their lives and something bigger, a grand purpose or scheme to which they can contribute. When we help our children discover God and His plan for their lives and they connect to Him, they embrace something bigger than their own lives. God's plans and purpose have eternal implications for every person. True significance can only be identified in connection with Him.

Second, people who feel significant have discovered their personal abilities or gifts, and they use them to contribute to the fulfillment of the bigger plan to which they are connected. Just connecting to something bigger is not enough to define their significance. It must be accompanied by a sense of personal contribution. They must know that their personal contribution is important in the grand scheme of things.

Third, people who feel significant have had their talents and contributions validated by another person. Parents or other people of influence must validate their purpose and acknowledge that the gifts and abilities they have contribute to a bigger purpose in an important way. If a person has the first and second parts of significance, but never receives validation from people of influence in his life, he will struggle to believe the significance of his contribution, never fully accepting it.

THE PROCESS OF SEARCHING

Finding significance is a process that unfolds over time, often over a period of years. The process can be difficult, and if the person is rebellious it will be painful, maybe even tragic. Aware of this reality, some parents refuse to empower their children to search.

The prodigal son's father empowered his search for significance. When his son requested his inheritance, the father granted his request. We can only assume he knew that a lecture would not change his son's mind. The request was a part of his son's search for purpose and significance. The boy had determined that what he wanted could not be found in the shadow of his brother or in the confines of the family business. So the father empowered his search.

The father empowered his son in two important ways. The first was financial empowerment through the provision of the son's inheritance. Why do you suppose the father would give his son an early inheritance? Would you suppose he had a clue as to how his son would use it? Surely if he had known, he would not have given it to his son to waste. Wouldn't a loving father have declined such a request?

The father's view of inheritance was different from the view of our western civilization. Our western view of an inheritance is that it is something we leave to our children to bless them with a better life. Using that logic, it makes no sense to give the inheritance when it will not be used to make a better life. That would be the majority opinion among parents today. But the father's attitude in the story was not the attitude of today. In that day an inheritance was something that was owed. It was an investment in his son's search for significance. If the father's investment resulted in his son finding purpose and significance, it would be a great investment, producing a result greater than any material accumulation an extra few years of waiting might produce.

The resource the son received in the form of his inheritance was secondary to the support he received in the form of his father's permission to fail in his search. When we as parents recognize our responsibility to help our children find significance, then investing in their search has a worthwhile purpose. By giving the inheritance with no conditions attached, the father acknowledged and empowered his son's freedom of choice.

Our children are not empowered to search if they cannot fail. I am not suggesting that failure is the best method for finding significance. Through years of investment, I have sought to guide my children in their search so that they would not have to hit rock bottom before finding their purpose. However, had they chosen the harder route, ignoring my guidance, I would have had to let them go.

Failure brought the prodigal son to an understanding of his own identity, gave him a desire to be connected to something bigger than himself, and helped him understand the value of being connected to family. The inheritance was wasted, but something greater was gained.

My dad did this for me when I was younger. He encouraged me to follow my heart, leave his company, and step into vocational ministry. Although it was not his plan for me to be in ministry, and even though it carried the risk of failure, my dad supported my decision and gave me the freedom to fail in my search.

EMPOWERMENT OR ENABLEMENT

How do we support our children's search for significance without it enabling their wrong behavior or poor choices? How do we provide resources and not compromise beliefs and values? If a child is not living or acting according to our standards, is the search invalidated or is this behavior a part of the searching process? These are important questions that must be answered so we know how to guide our children in their search.

In a positive sense, enablement and empowerment could be used synonymously. However, I want to talk with you for a minute about enablement that is negative and unhealthy, meaning it gives authority to do wrong through tacit approval of the values behind behavior. This enablement will not have a guiding result but in reality is negligent oversight.

Considering this definition of enablement, how would you respond to the following question? Is providing resource for your child's search for significance equal to, or the same as, approving his behavior? Is it the same as accepting his values? Or is it acknowledging his self-governance?

If supporting his search equates to approving wrong behavior or accepting alternative values as the foundation for determining behavior, then it would be irresponsible to give support. But is that right? Did the father in the story of the prodigal son give authority for his son's riotous living or accept his son's values for behavior by supporting his search? The answer is NO.

He empowered his son's search, but he did not enable his son's bad behavior and wrong choices by sending additional support when the son's funds ran out. Acknowledging his son's right and responsibility to govern himself, the father gave his son his inheritance and made him responsible for how it was spent.

Let me put this discussion in another context. If you encountered a homeless person on the street corner holding a sign that read, "Vet out of work. Need food. Can you spare some change?" and you felt compassion for the person and reached into your pocket and gave him some money, would your act of compassion give him authority to beg or associate you with his values for behavior? The answer is no. By responding with compassion to a need, you have neither automatically approved the

> *You should support your children's search for purpose and significance without enabling them in an unhealthy way.*

behavior, nor associated yourself with the values.

Consider another situation. You are an employer and you have an employee whose personal behavior away from work does not please you or represent your values. When you hand him his paycheck, are you agreeing with your employee's behavior away from your workplace or the values that form the basis for his actions? Again, the answer is no. When you hand him his paycheck, you are giving him something that is due him in exchange for the work he has done. When you give him his check, he is responsible for how it is spent; you are acknowledging his responsibility for self-governance.

We should support our children's search for purpose and significance without enabling them in an unhealthy way. When our support is a response that acknowledges their responsibility for self-governance, it is an empowering response. This is what our children need.

I grew up with an awareness that I was entitled to certain benefits just because I was born into the Lane family. The benefits were based upon my blood relationship, not upon my behavior. My dad often told me something like this: "If you rob a bank or murder someone, I am still going to love you. I will always love you. You will always be a part of this family. I may not like what you do, but you will always be my son."

Regardless of my behavior, my dad will always be my dad. That concept is a biblical concept as well. In fact, the whole idea of inheritance in the Bible is based on relationship, not merit. Consider for a moment the benefits your children are entitled to simply because they were born into your family, benefits such as unconditional love, security, food, clothing, etc. On top of these benefits, which are guaranteed to each family member, are conditional blessings, which are based upon approval and agreement with the choices and direction of the each individual family member.

There is practical wisdom I see in the father's response to his prodigal son's request that we can use for ourselves. First, when the search involves a departure from parental values, the financial support is for a defined amount. The father determined what was due his son in the amount of inheritance and gave it to him—no monthly support and no further response to the son when the money was gone.

When does support become unhealthy enablement for a child's behavior? When you give and it is wasted, and you give and it is wasted, and you continue to be an unending resource of material support, you are enabling your child's rebellion. His riotous lifestyle is no longer a search; it is a decision that has resulted in rebellion against you and God. To provide continued support for this behavior is enabling his rebellion and prolonging the process of him coming to his senses.

A Concluding Thought

The final thought I draw from the story of the prodigal son is this: *it is never too late to do what is right.* If you have a wayward child, he has been in God's care all along. You can begin today to release your child to find significance by freeing him from your criticism, threats of rejection, or attempts of control.

As you have read this chapter, you may have been convicted by the realization that you have not fulfilled your responsibility as a parent to help your child find identity and purpose through connection to God's sovereign plan for his life. It might be that throughout the discussion in this chapter, you have become aware of how little affirmation or support you have given your child in his search for personal significance. It is not too late. You can start today. Simply ask God to give you insight and wisdom on exactly what you should do. I know He will direct you and give you grace to accomplish this important work.

By faith, you can anticipate the completion of your child's search, believing God to bring him to his senses. During the process, I encourage you to hold celebration in your heart, and expect your child's return because, "it ain't over till its over!"

> *"Train up a child in the way he should go, And when he is old he will not depart from it."* Proverbs 22:6

CHAPTER 17

Partnering with God through Prayer

Prayer is the connective link between God and us. It is neither a religious duty, nor a pattern of sentence construction that dates back to the 18th century, nor is it something that can only be done by a member of the clergy. Prayer is a conversation with God that flows out of a relationship with Him.

Throughout the pages of this book, I have sought to share my philosophies and my experiences related to parenting. The bedrock of these philosophies is my conviction that parenting, at its core, is a partnership with God.

As a father, I am God's representative to my children. I am an extension and reflection of Him to them. If I am detached from my children, they see God as detached. If I act bored with them, they see God as bored with them. If I am present, involved, and interested, they will grow up with the correct perception of God. The kind of father I am forms the basis for my children's understanding of God's love and care.

Remember the story from Chapter One about the college professor's survey? After a whole semester of Bible study, the students' perceptions of God were still a *direct reflection* of their

To partner with God as His representative, you must pray.

relationships with their fathers! Nine weeks of instruction—27 classes of Bible teaching, homework, and tests—had not changed their perspectives. The students' home environments and the demonstrations of their fathers' love, or lack of it, was stronger than all the hours of teaching and study.

The impact of parents' influence on their children is profound—by God's design. He never intended for parenting to be a solely human endeavor. He designed parenting to be a partnership between Himself, the Divine Creator, and parents, His agents of procreation.

To be a partner with Him - to be His representative - we must pray.

Now, the subject of prayer can evoke a variety of thoughts, so let me briefly explain what I mean by prayer. Prayer is the connective link between God and us. It is neither a religious duty, nor a pattern of sentence construction that dates back to the 18th century, nor is it something that can only be done by a member of the clergy. *Prayer is a conversation with God that flows out of a relationship with Him.* Prayer is nothing more than conversation. Through prayer we communicate just as we would converse with anyone with whom we have relationship. As a father, I am motivated to pray because I know prayer is part of my responsibility as God's partner. Through prayer we communicate, God and I, about how to mold, nurture, and develop my children. Prayer waters and fertilizes the principles of life and qualities of character that I am planting deep into the fertile soil of my children's hearts.

Imparting the principles of God into life's learning situations is a process, much like the one a farmer goes through. To achieve the maximum results from his labor, a farmer must plant the right seed in the right season. If he doesn't plant seeds—in the right season— no crop will be produced. After he plants the seed, watering and

> *Prayer is the recognition and extension of your partnership with God to raise and influence your children.*

fertilizing will determine the quantity and quality of fruit produced.

As it is with crops, so it is with children. We must plant seeds in their lives. We must also realize that the quality and the quantity of the fruit produced in our children's lives will be determined by our attention to the process. Without watering and fertilizing the principles of God through patient application, watchful oversight, and prayer, the best results will not be produced.

In the case of the farmer, even though he picks the right crop and plants it at the right time, he must water and fertilize the crop or it will be stunted in its growth, producing little or no fruit. It is the same with our parenting: even though we are diligent to impart the right biblical principles, and we apply them with patient oversight, the effectiveness of our work will be diminished without prayer. Prayer waters the principles we teach into our children's hearts and makes sure that the greatest amount of fruit is produced. Without prayer, our effort will produce weak results. Prayer is the recognition and extension of our partnership with God to raise and influence our children in partnership with Him.

Where to Begin

As you read this book, you may have children who are elementary age or teenagers or adults with families of their own. No matter what their ages, it is never too late to start praying for them.

I love the statement of a preacher who opened his radio program with this phrase: "*God is still on the throne, and prayer changes things!*" That statement embodies the two foundational stones on which prayer is based.

"*God is still on the throne*" means that He is in control. No situation or circumstance is a surprise to Him or is beyond His power to change. "*Prayer changes things*" means that my petitions to God make a difference. God listens and responds to my requests.

How to Pray

When I pray for my children, I ask God to bless them, to lead them into the fullness of His purpose for their lives, and to give me wisdom for decisions regarding them.

When Lisa, our oldest daughter was approaching her sixteenth birthday she began lobbying for a car. We told her that we would pray with her about a car. After we had been praying for a few weeks we were given a car for Lisa from a family member. Jan and I were thrilled by what we recognized as a answer to prayer. Lisa was less than thrilled, she was thinking of something different than a 1985 Pontiac 4-door sedan that only had an AM radio. She acted like it would be better to walk than drive a, "old person's" car.

Her attitude probably reflects what most teens would feel in her situation if they felt they had a choice of what car they were going to drive. We gave Lisa our perspective on the car; that God had supplied the car for her and maybe the reason she got that particular car was to deal with an attitude of pride. We have taught and modeled for our children the belief that God's nature is to bless us, and it is His great joy to give us the desires of our heart. But He is first a good Father and will not give us a gift that would foster qualities or behavior that is harmful to us.

I told her I was convinced that God would not provide another car for her until she had changed her attitude and could demonstrate her change in the way she accepted and cared for the car God had supplied. To her credit she did change her attitude, and the pride that sought to make her hold her identity in a "thing," like the car.

Lisa drove that car for almost a year with a changed attitude. About a month before her seventeenth birthday, she asked if she and her mother could go look at a car she saw for sale in the paper. I told her yes, but not to get her hopes up about a new car. The car she looked at was a 1991 Red Mitsubishi Eclipse. She fell absolutely in love with the car and asked me if I would go with her to look at it and test-drive it, which I did. It was a cute car but it had high mileage, and the owner was asking too much for the car. As we drove home I told Lisa I did not feel that was the car for her. She was disappointed but understood.

Jan and I talked about getting Lisa another car and decided to call a friend in the auto body repair business to see if he had anything he was working on that might fit our need and budget. He said he had just finished one and he thought it would be perfect for a teenage girl and ask me to come have a look. The next day on my way home from work I went by his shop and out in front, shining in the fall sun, was a Red 1990 Mitsubishi Eclipse almost identical to the one Lisa and I test drove. This one had been in an accident and my friend had bought it and repaired the damage. It looked perfect.

I asked him if I could take it for a test-drive and if it would be all right to have a dealer check it out mechanically. He gave his okay. So Jan and I took it for a drive and then went to the dealer where we left it over night to be checked out. It all checked out great and we negotiated a sales price pleasing to us both. It was just 2 days before Lisa's birthday, so I took the car back to the dealer for them to change the oil and give it a tune-up.

I picked it up after work on the night of her birthday. We had planned a birthday dinner with the family. I pulled up in front of the house and parked in the driveway. I casually walked in the front door and yelled up the steps to Lisa (all the other family members waiting in hiding). I asked her to come down stairs for a minute, and as she made her way down the steps I told her I had something for her out front. She jumped the remaining few steps onto the floor and out the door. When she saw the car she stopped dead in her tracks. She started jumping up and down, screaming of course, by this time all the family was out in front to see the presentation and Lisa's reaction. She ran to the car dancing a full circle around it screaming and shouting the whole time. Then she ran to Jan and I with hugs of joy and excitement. God had given her the desire of her heart. There was just an interim step in the process. He had answered her prayer and ours—while correcting an attitude of pride in her heart.

I started praying like this for my children when they were young and continue to pray blessing over them even now that they are adults. As my children have matured through the stages of life, my prayers have changed accordingly. For instance, when they were born, they were in their most dependent stage of life. I would pray over them as I rocked them to sleep, asking God to give them good health and strength all the days of their lives. My prayers would be for their heart to always be turned toward God so that they never walk in rebellion against Jan and me or against God. I asked for wisdom and guidance to be a good parent and to teach my children the ways of God. I asked for God's help to live before my children as a model of consistent and genuine love for God, even as I expressed my love for them. I asked Him to show me His will for my life and to enable me to be obedient to His leading as a model for my children to follow.

As my children matured, prayer covered every situation they encountered. Problems with friends, academic struggles, teacher difficulties, personality and attitude problems were all covered in prayer. Opportunities, such as trying out for an athletic team, for a starting position, for cheerleader, for choir, or applying for jobs were all covered in prayer. The older our children became, the greater their needs—in a dollar sense as well as a spiritual sense. We prayed for emotional, physical, spiritual, and financial needs, no matter what they were. Because of prayer, God has provided college tuition and vehicles when we had no way to supply those things, opened doors of opportunity, and protected our children from physical harm.

In these situations, our human perspective is so limited. It is

> *In His all-knowing wisdom,*
> *He sees opportunities in the light*
> *of His purpose for my children, and*
> *He knows which ones will lead to the*
> *fulfillment of that purpose.*

easy to measure each circumstance by its immediate impact, but there is so much more to be considered, so much more that I do not know. For instance, if my child makes the team, and if he becomes a starter, what will be the affect of this opportunity? What influences will he be subjected to? Will he be strong enough to stand amidst these influences or will he be led astray? The answer to these questions lies outside my knowledge as a parent, but not outside of God's infinite knowledge. That is what He is all about, so I can cast my cares upon Him because I am convinced He cares for me and for my children! I pray for opportunities and ask God to direct the outcome as He knows best.

Some opportunities that I think are awesome, that I think will be wonderful and positive, He may see differently, knowing their future effect. Opportunities that never materialize (that I want to materialize because I think they would be a positive) may not materialize because He has other plans that do not include the particular opportunity at hand. Some opportunities never materialize because He knows the results the opportunities will produce. In His all-knowing wisdom, He sees opportunities in the light of His purpose for my children, and He knows which ones will lead to the fulfillment of that purpose and which ones will not.

We must trust the outcome of situations we hold in prayer into His care. Prayer requires trust and confidence in our partnership. *God will uphold His end of the partnership!* Don't be hesitant or embarrassed to pray. In real terms, prayer is communication with our Partner in parenting.

Prayer Journal

When my children were newborns, I prayed over them as I rocked them to sleep. As my children have matured into adults, I have begun keeping a journal of my personal prayer life. I wish I had known about keeping a prayer journal sooner. It would not have changed my prayers, but would have enhanced them.

Keeping a prayer journal has accomplished two important things in my prayer life. First, it has served as a reminder of the consistency of my praying. I date my entries into the journal, so if I miss multiple days, it is documented. When I did not journal, I had no record of the consistency of my prayer effort. Please understand that I do not view prayer from a legalistic perspective; I do not feel guilty if I miss a day in my journal. I consider my prayer journal as a reminder, like a close friend, who would remind me if we did not talk in several days. The journal produces a longing and a reminder to stay in touch, as I would with a phone call to a loved one or friend. The longing then leads to an effort to communicate more frequently because I care.

Secondly, keeping a prayer journal allows me to document the things I am praying for. Through my journal, I have a tangible way to keep track of specific prayers, along with the answers and direction I receive from God. It provides a way to reflect back over a span of time, on what God has done through my prayers. Keeping a journal helps foster a heart and an attitude of gratitude as I realize

God's faithfulness to answer my prayers.

Remember the story in Chapter 6 about Lisa and her boyfriend, and the word God gave me for her to wait on a match made-in-heaven? Here's how that played out in my journal:

You'll recall that our oldest daughter, Lisa, was in her freshman year of college at the University of Nebraska in Omaha. She had developed a serious interest in a young man she was dating. Jan and I were concerned about the relationship, but we knew it was between Lisa and God.

One morning as I was praying, Lisa came to mind. I felt God speak to my heart. He said Lisa was okay, but He had a promise for her. Here is the entry from my journal:

> January 22, 1996—As I was thinking and praying for Lisa, I felt the Lord put this impression on my heart for Lisa. The Lord said, "I am preparing a husband for Lisa, and he will fulfill all her desires, and he will love Me first—with all his heart. Tell her I am preparing a husband for her, and he will be everything she desires. Tell her not to compromise her desires in order to get a husband. I will provide her with one that will fulfill all her desires!"

A short time later, I called Lisa and, as we talked, she told me she was trying to decide what to do with her relationship with this young man. I thought how timely was the word the Lord gave me! I told Lisa what God had spoken to me in my prayer time. There was no pressure on my part, or an attempt to manipulate her with a spiritual message. I simply gave her an encouraging message from God spoken right to her heart. It was her choice whether to receive the message as from God. It was to encourage her faith at a critical point. She did take it as God's message to her leading her to re-evaluate her relationship with the young man she was dating. Shortly thereafter, the relationship with this young man ended.

During the next two years, Lisa would occasionally say to me, "Dad, remind me what God said in the word about my husband." I would go back and reference my journal to recount to her exactly what I heard and wrote the day I received it in my prayer time. Two years went by. Lisa had transferred to Baylor University in Waco, Texas, and she was home for the Thanksgiving holiday.

While she was home, a group of singles from the church came to our house to hangout and play games. A young man there that night caught Lisa's eye. They spent quite a bit of time together before she went back to school. Through separate experiences, the Lord spoke to Jan and me both that this young man was the man He had prepared for Lisa. More than two years had passed since I had received that word written in my journal, and it would involve another thirteen months of dating to complete the Lord's work in both of them before they would marry.

Partnering with God in His work of development in our children is exciting. Prayer is the essential link that facilitates our partnership. There are many examples of prayer I could share. Just as no two children are the same, the prayer needs of each child are not the same either. Our connection with our children establishes an awareness of their individual needs, and our partnership with God removes the burden of absolute responsibility from us and transfers it to Him. His yoke is not too burdensome, nor is it too heavy to carry. He is able to change and affect things that I cannot touch, even by a Herculean human effort. Prayer changes things!

Final Thoughts

I hope this chapter has encouraged you to partner with God, through prayer, in the development of your children. Partnering with God is not hard. Your personal worthiness has no bearing on it. Prayer is about communicating with Him to see that His purposes are accomplished in your children's lives. It is never too late to start, so don't worry if your kids are older and you have lost some developmental years. Even if your children are grown with children of their own, you can partner with God to see His purposes realized in every situation in your children and grandchildren.

The prayer of a father has great power to influence his children and beyond to future generations.

God is still on the throne and prayer changes things!

ENDNOTES

[1] United States Holocaust Memorial Museum, Washington, D.C. Holocaust article, www.ushmm.org.

[2] New York City (pop. 7.3 million), Los Angeles (3.5 million), Chicago (2.7 million), Houston (1.7 million), and Philadelphia (1.4 million). Source: U.S. Census 1990.

[3] Gallup Poll.

Determine Your Future by the Words You Speak Today

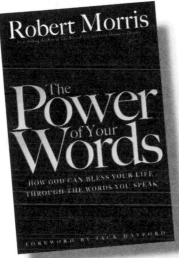

The Power of Your Words

In *The Power of Your Words*, Robert Morris tells us that there are three types of people: (1) those who think *before* they speak; (2) those who think *while* they speak; and (3) those who think *after* they speak. Which one are you? If you were told that God records every word you speak, would this help you to think before you speak?

We all know that words carry enormous power—the power to heal or to wound, to encourage or to dishearten, to speak truth or to deceive, to praise or to criticize. They can be the key to our success or the reason for our downfall. So, how do we harness that power? How do we learn to use our words to their greatest potential?

The Power of Your Words will take you on a journey of discovery into more than just the obvious physical and emotional impact your words can have; this is a journey that will help you understand the spiritual force inherent in every word you speak. Find out how to live more freely; how to connect more meaningfully; how to undo the damage of your words; and, most important, how to pause, ponder, and then pray before speaking.

Robert Morris wants you to know that good words last and carry enormous power to help, heal, encourage and move us to a greater level of living. When you say something positive or encouraging to your spouse, to your kids or to your friends, your words will last forever.

Dream to Destiny

Each of us is given a dream by God—it's the notion that sets our hearts racing at the mere thought of it. Unfortunately, most people never see their dream come to pass, so they never fulfill the destiny that God has in store for them. Robert Morris tells readers exactly how to make their dream into the reality for which they long. Using the example of Joseph in the Old Testament, Pastor Robert shows how God gave Joseph a dream and then promptly took him though 10 character-building tests that lasted 13 years. These tests assessed Joseph's strengths and weaknesses—form pride to purity—and they are the same tests that we all must pass before God will allow us to realize our dream.

Find out what the tests are and if you are passing or failing them, and get ready to begin fulfilling the destiny that God has in store for you.

The Blessed Life

This book will transform your life for the better, bringing you guaranteed financial results. But it will do more than that. It will change every area of your life: marriage, family, health and relationships. For when God changes your heart from selfishness to generosity, every part of your life-journey is affected.

If all believers followed the practical guidance of *The Blessed Life*, every church could be built, every nation would have an abundance of missionaries—and all would reap the benefits of having a generous heart. With humor, passion and clarity, Robert Morris presents the secrets of living a blessed life both financially and spiritually.

Pastor Robert Morris' books can be ordered at:
www.amazon.com

Resources to Help You Build a Healthy Marriage and a Stronger Family

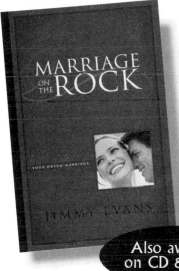

Marriage On The Rock

Now there is a book that gives you the key points to improving your marriage – making it the dream marriage you have always wanted. This 287-page book will show you the four foundational laws of marriage, tell you what the Bible says about the roles of husband and wife, and explain how to understand your spouse's needs. This book is a must for everyone wanting a successful marriage – a marriage built on the Rock – Jesus.

#BK01 Paperback Book
(287 pages)

#DVD01 5-DVD series

#CD011 5-CD series

Freedom From Your Past

Here is the Christian guide to personal healing and restoration. Based on the premise that the past isn't really the past until it has been reconciled in Christ, this book will show you how past attitudes can sabotage your future and how to heal the hurts and rejection from the past to live a victorious life now. *Freedom From Your Past* is packed full of useful tips and instructions to help you put your past behind you forever!

#BK05 Paperback Book
#CD47 6-CD series

Resources to Help You Build a Healthy Marriage and a Stronger Family

Emotionally Healthy Marriage

At last! A teaching that helps you understand the ups and downs of emotions and how to manage them effectively. Discover how to set realistic expectations in your marriage—how to meet the needs of your spouse and work through issues together, instead of frustrating each other. Learn how to resolve the issues of the past and how to determine emotional trouble spots.

#DVD41 2-DVD series
#CD41 4-CD series

The Keys to Sexual Fulfillment In Marriage

From creation, God intended married couples to enjoy sex. Yet today, as the entertainment industry distorts sexuality, God's intentions are misunderstood. As a result, many married couples experience frustration and hurt instead of finding the tremendous pleasure and fulfillment designed by God for marriage. This book will help!

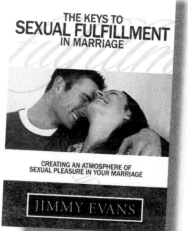

#BK11 Paperback booklet
(55 pages)

To order call 1 (800) 868-8349
www.marriagetoday.org
Marriage Today™ • P.O. Box 59888 • Dallas, Texas 75229